2295

Red and Blue God, Black and Blue Church

Red and Blue God, Black and Blue Church

Eyewitness Accounts of How American Churches Are Hijacking Jesus, Bagging the Beatitudes, and Worshiping the Almighty Dollar

Becky Garrison

FOREWORD BY ROBERT DARDEN

JOSSEY-BASS
A Wiley Imprint
www.josseybass.com

Published by Jossey-Bass
A Wiley Imprint
989 Market Street, San Francisco, CA 94103-1741   www.josseybass.com

Jossey-Bass books and products are available through most bookstores. To contact Jossey-Bass directly call our Customer Care Department within the U.S. at 800-956-7739, outside the U.S. at 317-572-3986, or fax 317-572-4002.

Jossey-Bass also publishes its books in a variety of electronic formats. Some content that appears in print may not be available in electronic books.

New Revised Standard Version Bible, copyright 1989, Division of Christian Education of the National Council of the Churches of Christ in the United States of America. Used by permission. All rights reserved.

Excerpts from Father Keating's *Crisis of Faith/Crisis of Love* reprinted by permission of the author and The Continuum International Publishing Group.

Excerpts from *Radical Hospitality: Benedict's Way of Love*, by Lonni Collins Pratt and Father Daniel Homan (© 2002 by Lonni Collins Pratt and Daniel Homan) used by permission of Paraclete Press.

Taken from *A Generous Orthodoxy* by Brian D. McLaren. Copyright © 2004 by Youth Specialties. Used by permission of The Zondervan Corporation.

Lyrics to "Jesus Loves Me But He Can't Stand You" (© 1991 by Don Peters) reprinted with permission of Don Peters.

Library of Congress Cataloging-in-Publication Data

Garrison, Becky, date.
    Red and blue God, black and blue church: eyewitness accounts of how American churches are hijacking Jesus, bagging the Beatitudes, and worshiping the almighty dollar / Becky Garrison; foreword by Robert Darden.
        p. cm.
    Includes bibliographical references and index.
    ISBN-13: 978-0-7879-8313-0 (cloth)
    ISBN-10: 0-7879-8313-6 (cloth)
    1. United States—Church history—21st century. 2. Christianity and politics—United States. 3. Christianity and culture—United States. I. Title.
    BR526.G37 2006
    277.3'083—dc22   2006000531

Printed in the United States of America
FIRST EDITION
HB *Printing*   10 9 8 7 6 5 4 3 2 1

Contents

This book is dedicated to my spiritual director,
the late Rev. Judith Tattersall Baumer,
who walked the walk and showed me
that I could be a believer without knowing all the answers.

Foreword

"I don't want you to go away with the impression
that there's any—you know—any inconveniences
involved in the religious life. I mean, a lot of people
don't take it up just because they think it's going to
involve a certain amount of nasty application and
perseverance—you know what I mean? . . . As soon
as we get out of chapel here, I hope you'll accept
from me a little volume I've always admired . . .
God Is My Hobby."

　　　　　　—*J. D. Salinger,* Franny and Zooey

Becky Garrison has written more articles, interviewed more people, and ruffled more feathers over the past twelve years for *The Wittenburg Door* than any single person, save our late founder Mike Yaconelli himself—and Mike had twenty years to accomplish the feat!

Unless you're another editor, what comes next won't interest you in the least and will veer dangerously close to being self-indulgent. Becky is that rarest of finds, an indefatigable investigator, researcher, and writer who takes chances and isn't afraid of being told no by a celebrity (or celebrity wannabe). I only have to make a suggestion once. Becky does not make the same mistake twice and (generally) accepts constructive criticism. She readily agrees to difficult assignments on short notice and generates her own interviews. She is relentless. She is irreplaceable. In short, every magazine ought to have a Becky Garrison.

But only one.

OK, if you're not the editor of a magazine, you can return to the Foreword now.

As I look back over Becky's dozens upon dozens of interviews for *The Door* (and various other publications), I'm struck by two things. First, the sheer diversity of the people she's bird-dogged until they've agreed to be interviewed by that most dangerous of all combinations—a religious humor and satire magazine with a lot of influence and a minuscule circulation when compared to "Christian" magazines like *Guideposts, Discipleship Journal,* and *Christianity Today.* A lose-lose proposition.

If you've heard of even half of the following names, consider yourself extremely knowledgeable and well read (and this is just a fraction of Becky's master interview list):

Steve Allen

Flip Benham

Lewis Black

William F. Buckley Jr.

Andrew Ferguson

Arianna Huffington

Molly Ivins

Jerry Jenkins

Dick Morris

Al Sharpton

Harry Shearer (voice of Rev. Lovejoy and Mr. Burns on
   The Simpsons)

Ron Sider

Miroslav Volf

Jim Wallis

Second, as I look over the humor pieces she's written for us, I'm struck by the subtle evolution I see reflected in her articles. The

style of humor, the subject matter, and the attack have all changed. Becky is living out her evolution as a writer and humorist (not necessarily the same thing, incidentally) in print. And perhaps even more significant, her humor journey reflects something of America's journey during the past twelve years or so.

I kid you not.

Several very fine books have documented the worldwide shift to conservatism (or fundamentalism), a phenomenon that has swept not just the Protestant and Catholic wings of Christianity but Islam, Judaism, and even Hinduism as well. Veteran politicians in a variety of countries, representing a host of religious beliefs, have bemoaned the crumbling of civility as this fundamentalist fervor has infected more and more governments, both civil and liturgical. The days of affable debate between candidates who actually liked each other—say, Dole and Clinton in the United States, for instance—is long gone, replaced by a dogmatic, Crusader mentality both here and abroad.

These are dangerous times we're living in.

In short, it's the perfect time to be a satirist!

Becky's own personal political and religious belief structure—conservative to moderate and at times, I dare say, liberal—has evolved as she's watched the bodies politic and the religious transform. It's reflected in what she writes. In fact, a few years ago, I accepted fewer of her humor pieces than I had previously, but not because they weren't as good as they used to be. They were better. But they had a harder edge, a more decidedly political slant.

That's troubling. You need the leavening of hope and redemption. *The Wittenburg Door* is, after all, a magazine that uses humor and satire to hold a mirror before the evangelical church. We dabble in politics *only* to the degree that those in power use religion to further their political ends.

Don't make me name names.

All editors want that level of passion in their writers. We want people who give a damn.

Fortunately, Becky's work has found that balance again. For satire to truly work, the satirist has to love the subject of his or her pen. You've got to care what happens to America, and you've got to care what happens to the church to write successful religious humor and satire. Without that love for your topic, it ain't satire—it's just a thinly disguised attack. It may be funny. But it isn't satire in the truest since of the word.

Becky loves the Church Triumphant and Universal, for all of its flaws. She cares about what happens to the United States of America, even if it currently happens to be the realm of Karl Rove.

Ultimately, there are several venues for creative people who feel this strongly about religion, race, the ecology, injustice, hunger, or whatever it is that floats your boat.

You can make powerful, life-changing (if essentially humorless) works of art. To wit:

Picasso's *Guernica*

The documentaries of Michael Moore

Rachel Carson's book *Silent Spring*

Peter Mullen's film *The Magdalene Sisters*

The songs of Bob Dylan or Billy Bragg or Bruce Cockburn

Or you can create passionate, vital works of faith, works that are inspired by your faith, which, by empowering people to live the Christian life to the fullest, thereby inspire them to make a difference. For instance:

The music and songs of John Rutter, Jan Krist, Russ Taff

The books of C. S. Lewis, J.R.R. Tolkien, Anne Lamott, Madeleine L'Engle

The art in the great cathedrals or the crosses of unnamed Celtic Christians

The insight of Thomas Merton or Julian of Norwich

The poetry of T. S. Eliot

In some rare cases, obviously, you can do both. But when you do neither of things but instead use religion as an excuse to produce second-rate dreck to sell to the burgeoning "Christian" market-place, well, now you're on *our* turf.

If we really believe that the Creator of the universe is the giver of all good gifts, then our gifts to the Creator shouldn't be pale imitations of the world's music, movies, books, art, or dance—they should be *better!*

Anything less is a sin.

Now *that*'s something to get fired up about. Watered-down, pale imitations of popular culture somehow made "better" or even—horrors!—*sanctified* by slapping "John 3:16" on them are abominations at worse, laughable at best.

You gotta laugh to keep from cryin'.

And that's what Becky has done.

Over the past decade or so, she's turned her considerable talents to carefully inspecting the Christian culture at large. Then—just as important—she's found a spot on a busy street corner and shouted, "Yo! People! THE EMPEROR IS *BUCK NEKKID!*"

That's what I like about this collection of essays.

Becky isn't afraid to speak truth to power. She usually does it in an abrasively funny way.

But then, truth—to be heard—often *must* be abrasive.

The truth hurts sometimes.

The end result of these observations is *Red and Blue God, Black and Blue Church: Eyewitness Accounts of How American Churches Are Hijacking Jesus, Bagging the Beatitudes, and Worshiping the Almighty Dollar.*

Yes, it's a mouthful.

But it'll make you laugh. It'll make you mad. It might even make you cry. And—in a perfect world—it might even make a difference.

If not, then by golly, this was *still* a noble effort, one inspired not by money (I don't know any rich religious humorist-satirists—hell, I don't know any *solvent* religious humorist-satirists) but by a burning conviction that has erupted into a full compulsion to write.

Hmmm . . . On second thought, that sounds a wee bit over the top.

Let's try a different approach.

This is good stuff, written by someone who cares deeply.

I recommend it to you.

No foolin'.

Waco, Texas   Robert Darden
March 2006   Senior Editor, *The Wittenburg Door*

Preface

It was the best of times, it was the worst of times, it was the
age of wisdom, it was the age of foolishness, it was the epoch
of belief, it was the epoch of incredulity, it was the season of
Light, it was the season of Darkness, it was the spring of
hope, it was the winter of despair, we had everything before
us, we had nothing before us, we were all going direct to
Heaven, we were all going direct the other way.
                    —*Charles Dickens*, A Tale of Two Cities

As Senior Contributing Editor for *The Wittenburg Door* for more than
a dozen years, I have become accustomed to slings and arrows, as well
as the occasional threatened lawsuit, hurled by the Religious Right
and the extreme left whenever our satire magazine implied that their
behavior was less than charitable—unchristian, if you will. Still, I
struggle to be faithful to *The Door's* mission, which is a scriptural
injunction to mock idolatry. The prophet Elijah did it best during his
contest with the priests of Baal. An expanded discussion of idolatry
can be found in the Talmud, that compendium of Jewish oral traditions that we find to be a continuing source of light on New Testament understanding. The rabbinic teachers said Israel was forbidden
to mock or jeer anyone or anything except idolatry. The prescribed
epigraph was "Take your idol and put it under your buttocks!" (as
translated on our Web site, http://www.wittenburgdoor.com).

   With this satirical mandate in mind, I have written *Red and Blue
God, Black and Blue Church: Eyewitness Accounts of How American*

Churches Are Hijacking Jesus, Bagging the Beatitudes, and Worshiping the Almighty Dollar. I hope this series of reflections will illuminate both the plank in the Religious Right's eye as well as the speck that blinds the Progressive Left. In its quest to get the "Christian vote," our two-party system has held Jesus' teachings hostage, with each side choosing only those select passages from Scripture that fulfill their partisan purposes. They damn anyone to hell (that's H-E-double toothpicks for all you Southern Baptists) that dare take issue with their political platforms. (I know, I know—I gotta work some more on that "judge not that you not be judged" bit.)

Alas, Jonathan Swift's words ring true today: "We have just enough religion to make us hate, but not enough to make us love, one another." Rather than engage with believers from different political backgrounds, all too often Christians confuse acceptance of others with approval of their position, refusing even to shake the hand of anyone whose political views do not meet with their explicit endorsement. And American Christians wonder why George Carlin and company consider us to be such (expletive deleted) hypocrites.

But the more that Christians can learn to mirror the love of Christ, who loved all humanity including His enemies, the more the church will truly reflect the body of Christ. *Red and Blue God, Black and Blue Church* focuses on the battles between the warring political factions. However, I also note those all too rare instances when instead of creating ideological havens for like-minded political souls to gather, the church has chosen to receive the other based on the Greatest Commandment of all. (In Appendix C, I list some positive resources that have helped me discern what it means to be a twenty-first-century Christian.) In Matthew 22:37–39, Jesus commands His disciples to "love your neighbor as yourself." This radical love extends to all of humanity, including one's political enemies. I am pleading with U.S. churches to end this infighting. Didn't we learn diddly from the Crusades, the Salem witch trials, or *Monty Python's Life of Brian?*

We all have our different worship preferences, ranging from high church to low church and even no church. We're never going to all want to go to the same church anyway. If we all did every-thing in exactly the same way, life would be boring beyond belief. But let's pray for that day when red and blue Christians can come together in communion as brothers and sisters in Christ.

New York, New York   Becky Garrison
March 2006

Introduction

Church Makes God Look Ridiculous
—*Landover Baptist Church bumper sticker*

I confess that like the late Mike Yaconelli, founder of *The Wittenburg Door,* I too have a "messy spirituality." I don't have all the answers, and I struggle with how to live out my faith, especially when it comes to voting my conscience in a post-Watergate world. When I got my voting card at the tender age of eighteen, I tried to carry on my late parents' legacy of political activism by campaigning for John Anderson. For those of you under the age of forty, Anderson was a ten-term Republican from Illinois who shook up the system by running for president as a moderate independent on the Unity Party platform in 1980.

While I bonded with the Wake Forest University Students for Anderson during our quest to "make a difference," my subsequent efforts to assist in a variety of local and national political campaigns in the early 1980s lacked the commitment, integrity, and creative mind expansiveness that I remember from my parents' days of giving their all for RFK, MLK, and LSD.

By 1988, I had pretty much checked myself out of the political process, save for my brief foray into the Young Republicans. Hey, don't knock it—those dudes were the party animals during the Reagan era.

As we approached a new millennium, I was facing a new frontier—a political landscape seemingly created by Warner Bros.

that offered me a choice between voting for either Yosemite Sam on the right or Foghorn Leghorn on the left. So I ended up doing what any red-blooded American would do: I cast a write-in vote for Snoopy. (OK, I confess. I actually ended up voting for Ralph Nader, but only because I wanted to try to light a stick of dynamite under our stagnant two-party system.)

Since the fateful day when Bush claimed his virtuous victory in 2000 by apparently breaking one of the commandments (stealing is, after all, still one of the top ten no-nos), conservative and progressive Christians have been dukin' it out *Dukes of Hazzard* style. We experienced a brief cease-fire in the war between the Religious Right and the Progressive Left on 9/11, when the nation came together following the terrorist attacks. As a volunteer at Ground Zero, I watched as rescue workers and volunteers at the World Trade Center site transformed into the universal church. People responded immediately and unflinchingly to the needs of strangers, giving freely of their time and talents without the expectation of receiving anything in return.

But while some souls continued to serve behind the scenes, a sizable minority of religiously minded folks, representing a wide range of 9/11 ministries, resumed their ideological turf battles. As the recovery effort progressed, too many Christians on both sides of the political spectrum were fighting for the soul of America and their own place in the media spotlight. Hell, all we needed to do was throw some lions in, and we could have had that Coliseum thingee all over again. But let's not and say we did.

> Religious controversies are always productive of more acrimony and irreconcilable hatreds than those which spring from any other cause.
>
> —George Washington

Supreme Court Justice Potter Stewart will long be remembered for the comment he made when he declined to define hard-core pornography, in response to a 1964 ruling: "I know it when I see it." Like Stewart, I know un-Christlike behavior when I see it. Despite all the talk about the Religious Right, the spiritual left, and the search for moral values, frankly, all too often these days Christians' behavior toward each other is anything but Christlike.

The conservative battle cry hit a fevered pitch on July 1, 2004, when Jerry Falwell sounded the marching orders for the Religious Right in his e-mail newsletter and on his Web site: "It is the responsibility of every political conservative, every evangelical Christian, every pro-life Catholic, every traditional Jew, every Reagan Democrat, and everyone in between to get serious about reelecting President Bush." Righteous Republicans across the country took up this Falwellian call to arms, transforming the Republican National Convention into an evangelistic extravaganza akin to a 700 Club telethon, complete with prominent displays of folks with televangelist-styled hair who praised Jesus, godly graphics, and a closing altar call. That was when the fundamentalist faithful once again anointed Bush adviser and political mastermind Karl Rove as the new Moses, the one who would take the Republican Party into the Promised Land.

However, a number of troubling and unresolved issues caused many a voter to ponder if reelecting Bush-Cheney was indeed a wise and just move. The U.S. economy was tanking. The Abu Ghraib prison scandal photos were being splashed all over the world, the 9/11 hearings suggested that the U.S. government knew a heck of a lot more than it was letting on, and the Bush twins' drunken antics were wearing thin. So one would think that any opponent who possessed even a modicum of political skill and a minimal degree of moral authority should have been able to capitalize on those problems and defeat Dubya. But as Jon Stewart, host of Comedy Central's Daily Show, pointed out, "You've got Senator Kerry, who's like Gore but without, you know, all the charisma." Throughout the election, this casual Catholic failed to articulate a clear moral vision on issues such as poverty, Iraq, and the environment, and his frequent flip-flopping became the butt of endless jokes on the late-night talk shows.

Even though I voted for Bush the Elder in 1988 and 1992, by 2004 I was so frustrated with his son that I would have voted for a dead dog on the side of the road over Dubya. But I wish my choice had been anyone other than a zombie from *The Night of the Living Dead*. Trying to decide if I wanted to vote for Kerry or W was akin to asking me if I'd prefer to have a cold or pneumonia. Where are folks like Christie Todd Whitman, Nelson Mandela, or Bono when you really need them?

Call to Renewal, a national network of churches, faith-based organizations, and individuals working to overcome poverty in America, headed by Jim Wallis, decried the partisan nature of the 2004 election by launching a campaign called "God Is Not a Republican. Or a Democrat." Unfortunately, too many churches chose to align themselves with a particular party platform rather than asking why neither political party was paying any real attention to the teachings of Christ when it comes to issues like poverty and the environment. Instead of preaching the Word of God, some religious leaders from both the conservative and the liberal ends of the spectrum chose to placate their favorite politicians.

"Political analysts and theologians say one thing is clear: Despite pre-election talk of war, terrorism and the economy, moral values became the lightning rod that mobilized voters in the 2004 election—some say at the expense of the church's autonomy because of its willingness to become a political player." That insightful comment was posted on the United Methodist Church's Web site. The followers of Methodist church founder John Wesley are right: when a church becomes subject to the whims of a political party's wishes, it loses its prophetic voice to proclaim the truth. Tony Campolo, a spiritual counselor to President Bill Clinton, echoed these concerns when he quoted a former mayor of Indianapolis in his book *Speaking My Mind:* "When you get the government involved with religious programs like this [referring to faith-based initiatives], it's like mixing horse manure with ice cream. It won't do much damage to the horse manure, but it will really mess up the ice cream." The Homer Simpsons of the world will say, "Ice cream . . . mmmmm" and eat whatever is put in front of them, but my hope is that for most of us, this combo makes us sick.

On Election Day 2004, 51 percent of Americans voted for Bush, and by midnight, pharmacies throughout the Northeast reported shortages of Tylenol. I watched as this massive national headache began to affect the church at the local level, resulting in a clash of primary colors. According to the liturgical church calendar, the color blue signifies Advent, the coming of Christ into the world, and the color red symbolizes Pentecost, which commemorates the descent of the Holy Ghost upon the Apostles. However, following the 2004 election, those colors represented political alliances rather than liturgical seasons. Churches had become blue and red houses of worship, where like-minded individuals went to affirm their political convictions and fine-tune their battle tactics against their alleged fellow Christians. Meanwhile, I was seeking in vain, it seemed, to find a gathering of faithful believers who try to live out the teachings of Christ by demonstrating His love toward the political stranger in their midst.

Around this time, I was attending a socially prominent, albeit progressive, mainline Episcopal church. I was having serious reservations about the United States' involvement in the Iraq war. (Eureka! I finally found one issue where I agree wholeheartedly with the pope!) However, I became perplexed when all too often, I would find scattered on the church's "welcoming table" pamphlets that engaged in vitriolic attacks against the Bush administration but were devoid of any spiritual substance.

Even though a few vestry members told me that we should pray for Bush and welcome him into our midst, when I posed the question, "Would you take communion with the president?" the collective answer from the congregation was a resounding "Hell no! We won't go!" and other slogans stolen from the sixties. So I knew I had to find another spiritual home, one that rooted its ministry in the liberating words of the Gospel and not in an outdated political platform that, frankly, was blowin' in the wind.

Since the 2004 election, my quest to find a church that both embraces the social gospel and welcomes me as a wandering Christian into its midst has resembled a Monty Python–esque search for the Holy Grail. Most mainline churches I entered either never bothered to follow up on the "visitor information" card I filled out or inundated me with stewardship stuff, so I crossed them off my list immediately. (The mainline churches' bewildering lukewarm attitude toward potential new members and their pay-to-pray stewardship tactics are topics for other books.)

Unfortunately, it seemed that just about every liberal Protestant church I entered required that I swear allegiance to the Democratic Party before I could be admitted into its inner sanctuary. While the more conservative churches welcomed me with open arms in accordance with Jesus' commandment to love one another, their venomous anti-DNC rants sent me running for the hills. They seemed to forget that Jesus Christ was in fact one helluva radical rule breaker and love maker. Finally, I found a few small havens where I could hang ten with God and leave my voting card at home. But I continue to wonder why these warm, inviting, and nonpartisan churches are so few and far between.

> You can tell you've created God in your own image if he or she hates all the same people you do.
> –Anne Lamott, *Plan B: Further Thoughts on Faith.*

How can we as a Christian community hope to come to any common ground and engage in civil discourse if we do not extend Christ's love to everyone, including those of different political persuasions? Instead of issuing Christian fatwas, can we extend the hand of compassion and love to our fellow brothers and sisters? Hmmm. . . . Let's explore together how we might add to the Ten Commandments a new commandment that Jesus gave to his disciples. Just as He loved them, they also should love one another (see John 13:34).

These are the times that try men's souls.
—Thomas Paine, December 1776

Red and Blue God, Black and Blue Church

1

THE GREATEST
COMMANDMENT OF ALL

If you wanna be Christian, that's cool, but you should
follow what Jesus taught instead of how he got killed.
Focusing on how he got killed is what people did in the
Dark Ages, and it ends up with really bad results.
　　　　　　　　　　　　　—*Stan Marsh*, South Park

My parents brought me up to hate President Richard Milhous
Nixon. Now I don't mean a legitimate dislike over the Nixon
administration's involvement in Vietnam or an understandable disgust that Tricky Dick's personal paranoia led to Watergate. Rather, I
was taught pure, unadulterated hatred for a man that I later learned
was a practicing Quaker—a fellow Christian, if you will. Even
though my late father, the Rev. Dr. Karl Claudius Garrison Jr., was a
self-proclaimed progressive priest and professor, his group of peaceful quasi-religious hippies taught me to love everyone. Except, of
course, for the Establishment, da man, and of course, Republicans.

　　So as a young adult, I did what anyone does when raised by left-
wing extremists—I joined an adult Campus Crusade Bible study
and became a Young Republican. These religious Republicans stood
ready to embrace me, provided I was willing to join them in chant-
ing "Demonic Democrats" and other similar slogans. My tenure
with these two groups was short-lived after I professed my abject
horror at the rise of the Moral Majority and questioned whether
Reagan's trickle-down economics was simply a polite euphemism
for whizzing on the poor. Clearly, I wasn't their kind of true red,
white, and blue believer. I was an improper Christian.

Where Is the Love?

John Whitehead of the Rutherford Institute notes, "Christ's message of love does not square with much of what we hear coming from certain quarters of modern evangelism—a religion steeped in an 'us versus them' mentality." What happened to the concept of the Christian community as a unified body of believers? Author and pastor Brian McLaren states, "The name of Jesus, whose life and message resonated with acceptance, welcome, and inclusion, has too often become a symbol of elitism, exclusion, and aggression. This pains me, and I imagine it pains Jesus too, who was himself Jewish and knew what it felt like to be treated with disdain."

As McLaren points out, this hatred of the other is nothing new. At the time of Jesus' birth, the Samaritans and the Jews had been at each other's throats for literally hundreds of years. At the time when Jesus told the parable of the Good Samaritan (see Luke 10:25–37), the concept of a Samaritan coming to the rescue of a Jew would have been considered just as incongruous as if, say, a Focus on the Family follower marched in the New York City LGBT (Lesbian, Gay, Bisexual, and Transgender) Pride Parade today. But as the parable made clear, the Samaritan was considered the Jewish man's "neighbor." By implication, that means the definition of "neighbor" has to be expanded to include all of God's children, including those of different social classes, races, creeds, and even political affiliations.

> Man is the only religious animal . . . that loves his neighbor as himself, and cuts his throat if his theology isn't straight.
>
> —Mark Twain, *Letters from the Earth*

When Jesus commanded His followers to "go and do likewise" by following the example of the Good Samaritan, he challenged the early church to look beyond its comfort zone. His disciples were required to obey the Greatest Commandment by showing His love and kindness to *all* people, because everyone was their "neighbor" (see Matthew 22:37–40 and Mark 12:28–31). The early Christian church cut across the various hierarchical lines that divided people. It did not seek to dominate the political establishment or maintain the status quo; rather its goal was to spread the universal love of Christ. In doing that, it transformed the world.

Pat Preaches

Unfortunately, the words of the Greatest Commandment have been repeated ad nauseam to the point where the radical message of Christ has been lost in our "yeah, right" cynical culture. Sometimes this cynicism is warranted. For instance, let's take a look at the pronouncements of televangelist Pat Robertson. In his teaching on the Greatest Commandment, Robertson proclaims that "a person must dedicate the totality of his being to a self-giving love for God. Every aspect of his nature must focus on loving God."

Say what? I mean, is this the same Pat Robertson who in August 2005 issued a Christian fatwa against a democratically elected world leader? I would challenge anyone to tell me what is "loving" about declaring to a worldwide televised audience that "if [Venezuelan President Hugo Chavez] thinks we're trying to assassinate him, I think we really ought to go ahead and do it." Robertson later apologized, but halfheartedly. He tried to weasel out of it by claiming that he didn't really say we should assassinate him but that our "special forces should take him out." Millions of viewers who saw the show or a tape of that segment know exactly what he said—that it would be cheaper to assassinate Chavez than to wage a costly war against him. But no matter how you slice this baloney, God makes it pretty clear that vengeance is his business and not ours (see Romans 12:19–21). In a few brief moments, Robertson managed to flush over two thousand years of Judeo-Christian teachings down the toilet.

As I witnessed that notorious segment on *The 700 Club*, my "judge that you not be judged" button got jammed. I'm trying to fix it, but it keeps short-circuiting on me. Maybe I'm not being Christlike, but I get pretty ticked when a brother in Christ suggests that it's OK to kill people who cause us political grief. Then again, this is the same dude that made this comment: "If I could just get a nuclear device inside Foggy Bottom [meaning the State Department], I think that's the answer." Clearly, his most recent assassination comment wasn't the first time he has suggested that murder could represent a viable solution, even if he meant it in jest.

Let's see how Pat Robertson demonstrates his love for his fellow brothers and sisters in Christ. According to Pat, "You say you're supposed to be nice to Episcopalians, Presbyterians, and Methodists. . . . Nonsense. I don't have to be nice to the spirit of the Antichrist."

There are those who would disagree with Robertson's picks for who embodies the spirit of the Antichrist. Fellow televangelist Robert Tilton declared Ole Anthony, founder of Trinity Foundation, to be the Antichrist. Then you have the Sex Pistols, who state that they are an Antichrist, as does "Antichrist Superstar" Marilyn Manson and lots of other wannabe satanist rockers. Also, just about every world leader who opposes the United States tends to get tagged "the Antichrist." Seems to me that certain religious leaders might be using this term a bit too loosely. I mean, some people who have been called the Antichrist, like Hitler and Saddam Hussein, are truly evil, but we're talking here about the epitome of evil, the baddest of the bad. When it comes to discerning just who is going to duke it out with Christ when the Second Coming hits, it seems to me it would help if we were all on the same page.

But guys like Pat never seem to let facts get in the way of a good story. For instance, how many people know that Robertson ain't a reverend? He likes to put on the posture of being a preacher, but he gave up his ordination as a Baptist minister in 1988 when he decided to run for president. I can see where people would still make the honest mistake and call him "Reverend Robertson." As host of *The 700 Club*, he prays for healing (provided your faith overrides your sense of reason and you funnel your fortunes into his pocket). And even though he's a layman, he preaches his interpretation of the Word of God to an average of one million American viewers daily. Some viewers, like me, watch Pat & Co. for comic relief and research purposes, but many people take this man's ramblings seriously or else he wouldn't be so filthy rich.

Though Robertson seems to be cuckoo for Christ, even he acknowledges that there are consequences to not following Jesus' teachings. He states, "A person would break the great commandment if his spirit was partially centered on making money to the exclusion of God."

Now, let's just see how well Pat puts this teaching into practice. Although I can never claim to know what's in someone's heart, it seems to me, at least on paper, that Robertson really, really likes making money. Lots of money. According to British journalist Greg Palast, Pat has a net worth estimated at between $200 million and $1 billion, a fortunate he amassed through moneymaking ventures including African gold and diamond mines, the Kalo-Vita vitamin pyramid scheme, the Bank of Scotland, the Family Channel, and the Ice Capades, as well as Age-Defying shakes, antioxidants, and protein pancakes. So is Pat guilty of not practicing what he preaches? Anyone who tunes in to more than a minute of *The 700 Club* can figure out pretty quickly that Pat's application of the Greatest Commandment does not extend to those godless heathen Democrats, feminists, and other political infidels that dare to thwart what *Fortune* magazine terms his "quest for eternal life." Lest you think I am exaggerating here, check out the dude's 1992 best-selling book *The New World Order* for a complete description of what the world would be like if Robertson ruled it.

> If we were really biblical, our agenda would cut sharply across the issues.
> —Ron Sider, president, Evangelicals for Social Action

As I've just noted, Pat's a good talker, but it's no wonder we're in such a mess—while guys like him are PR geniuses when it comes to talking the talk, they appear to be walking away from Christ's teachings.

Putting Principles into Practice?

The National Association of Evangelicals (NAE) created a position paper, "For the Health of the Nation: An Evangelical Call to Civic Responsibility," to explore the religious-political mess we're in these days. This document was created by two dozen scholars who bridged the spectrum of conservative to liberal evangelical thought encompassed by the organization's forty-five thousand churches, which represent fifty-two denominations. Among the signers of this document we find such luminaries as James Dobson, chairman of Focus on the Family; Richard Land, president of the Ethics and Religious Liberty Commission of the Southern Baptist Convention; Charles Colson, president of the Prison Fellowship ministry; and Rick Warren (the *Purpose Driven Life* dude). We're talking about the big guns here.

According to this document, "We will differ with other Christians and with non-Christians over the best policies. Thus we must practice humility and cooperation to achieve modest and attainable goals for the good of society. We must take care to employ the language of civility and to avoid denigrating those with whom we disagree." I dunno about you, but I'm not seeing too much coming from Colorado Springs, home of Focus on the Family Ministries, that strikes me as humble and civil. If you know what I mean—and I think you do.

Ted Haggard, founder and pastor of New Life Church in Colorado Springs and president of both the NAE and the World Prayer Team, talks once a week to President Bush. If Ted, as NAE president, by any chance emphasizes to the president the importance of putting these principles into practice, it doesn't exactly show; "cooperation" isn't the word that comes to mind to describe the Bushies' treatment toward those with whom they disagree. Is George W. Bush ignoring Ted Haggard's pastoral guidance when it comes to those "difficult" parts of the Greatest Commandment? In his case, that means the need to extend Christ's love all of humanity, including those pesky liberal Democrats.

Broadcasting the Good News?

As a working journalist, I often hear about interfaith peace walks, prayer services, community service days, and other gatherings that are designed as an opportunity for genuine fellowship, but these events seldom, if ever, get any media attention. Yes, having Jews, Christians, and Muslims holding hands together in solidarity isn't as titillating as watching Christians cat-fighting *Crossfire*-style, spotting a disgraced televangelist or a pedophile priest doing a perv walk, or witnessing footage of a Jewish community center that's been defaced with swastikas. But why is there this overexposure on the underbelly of the faith community? What if the glare of the media spotlight were refocused to show the Good News at least every once in a while?

(By the way, I admit that in my work for *The Wittenburg Door,* I definitely slam those who follow their own self-interests rather than following the commandments of Christ, but if you read my interviews, you'll see that I do profile those that walk the walk as well. So I try to be a bit balanced here. But I confess that this can be a challenge, mainly because the bad stuff is just so durn juicy. Also, most church-related press material puts me to sleep before I finish reading it.)

I wonder what our nation's capital would be like if every politician who accepted a campaign contribution from one of the 110 million or so Americans who support the NAE decided to follow the principles advocated in this document. Imagine what would happen if they all stop bickering about displaying the Ten Commandments and focused instead on living out the Greatest Commandment.

Conversely, many progressives continue my late father's legacy of loving all humanity except when it comes to their conservative brothers and sisters in Christ. Take, for example, the New York Open Center, an organization that describes itself as New York City's leading center for holistic learning and culture. It joined forces with the National Council of Churches of Christ USA, People for the American Way, the *Village Voice*, *The Nation*, and Americans United for Separation of Church and State to sponsor a post-2004 election conference titled "Examining the Real Agenda of the Religious Far Right." This daylong event included seminars with topics like "Christian Jihad" and "Is an Unholy American Theocracy Here?" Hmmm . . . methinks they are open more to ridicule than to serious debate, since this warlike language makes me wonder just who is included in their seemingly "open" society. If this group practiced true openness by engaging in constructive dialogue with its perceived "enemy" about Jesus' teachings on specific social issues instead of engaging in name-calling, it might just get somewhere.

According to its brochure, the Faith and Politics Institute provides Congress with opportunities for moral reflection and spiritual community, drawing universal wisdom from a range of religious traditions. Through its conferences, seminars, and retreats, this institute strives to strengthen political leadership that contributes to healing the wounds that divide the nation and the world. This effort has attracted the attention of leaders including Senate Majority Leader Bill Frist, a Republican from Tennessee and a medical doctor; the internationally renowned Buddhist monk Thich Nhat Hahn; Anglican Archbishop Njongonkulu Ndungane of South Africa; and House Democratic Leader Nancy Pelosi of California.

I, for one, am encouraged by the sight of religious leaders and political luminaries lending their support to an interfaith movement that encourages members of Congress to pray and listen to one another. But frankly, based on what I've witnessed on Capitol Hill, I'm wondering just how many congressmen and staff members who participate in these programs actually implement these principles. These days, I feel like I'm witnessing a full-scale war of words as Christians on both sides of the political spectrum blast their opponents to bits instead of attempting to come together in prayer as fellow believers asking for God's guidance. The Dalai Lama offers these words of wisdom: "Unfortunately, love and compassion have been omitted from too many spheres of social interactions for too long. Usually confined to family and home, their practice in public life is considered impractical, even naïve. This is tragic."

Radical Love in Action

Martin Luther King Jr. keenly observed that the very center of Jesus' teachings focused on the need to love one's enemy. "Hate for hate only intensifies the existence of hate and evil in the universe," he said, adding that somebody must have enough religion and morality to cut off this hatred and inject that strong and powerful element of love within the very structure of the universe. As Candace Chellew-Hodge, founder of *Whosoever*, an online magazine for gay, lesbian, bisexual, and transgender Christians, points out, "The political implications of this message are enormous. If the hearts and minds of the people are changed and they demand that people love their neighbor as they love themselves and they begin to design society in that manner, then naturally their government will change."

During Habitat for Humanity's 2000 Jimmy Carter Work Project held in New York City, I saw this love in action as former President Jimmy Carter and New York City Mayor Rudy Giuliani proved that at least for a moment, a Southern Baptist and a Roman Catholic from opposing political parties could work together toward the common goal of providing affordable housing. Throughout this week's festivities, I experienced a bit of the kingdom here on earth as people of all faiths from across the country came together to help families achieve the dream of home ownership.

As Christians, we are brothers and sisters in Christ, and that means we're a family. In all but the

We work side by side with poor families who will be able to own the houses because Habitat follows the biblical prohibition against charging interest. This has been an enjoyable and heartwarming experience for us and many others to put our religious faith into practice, and it demonstrates vividly the importance and difficulty of reaching out to needy people.
    –Jimmy Carter, *Our Endangered Values*

Unless you know how to love your neighbor, you cannot love God. Before placing an offering on the altar of God, you have to reconcile with your neighbor, because reconciling with your neighbor is to reconcile with God.

–Thich Nhat Hahn, *Taming the Tiger Within*

most dysfunctional of families, there is some degree of love extended toward others in the family, even though you may hate their guts at any given moment. Heck, while I seriously doubt that Dick Cheney will ever don a rainbow-colored Parents and Friends of Lesbian and Gays (PFLAG) T-shirt, unlike some conservatives who shun their homosexual children, he has made it clear that he loves his lesbian daughter, though he disapproves of her lifestyle.

If you claim to be a Christian, you must love even those whose political views you may despise, for they too are children of God and part of the Christian family. That means no hurling nasty epithets toward those with whom you disagree, even if your comments contain a grain of truth.

Loving your neighbor doesn't mean you should turn a blind eye to your neighbor's behavior. Actions like beating the bejeezus out of POWs, depriving God's children of food and shelter, or telling Mother Earth to go take a hike clearly go against Gospel teachings. By all means, examine the policies advanced by politicians who claim to be speaking for Christ to see if their pronouncements reflect the Gospel Truth or the whims of those who are bankrolling their campaigns. But when you preach against ungodly behavior, pray about how to frame the discussion, so you are honing in on the policy and not the person. Disagree with what they say but continue to love them as brothers and sisters in Christ. It's that hate-the-sin-but-love-the-sinner business. Deal with it.

As a religious satirist, I have major problems trying to implement this commandment; I know from firsthand experience how difficult it can be to put Christ's radical love into daily practice. It seems next to impossible, but Jesus considered it our number one priority. That's why they call it the Greatest Commandment.

2

GUNS, GOD, 'N' GROUND ZERO

Lord, take me where You want me to go;
Let me meet who You want me to meet;
Tell me what You want me to say, and
Keep me out of Your way.
——*Mychal Judge, Catholic priest and chaplain*
for the Fire Department of New York

When asked to describe what the Kingdom of God is like, Jesus employs metaphors like a pearl, a mustard seed, or a banquet. For me, God is like the New York City firefighters who went into the Twin Towers of the World Trade Center on September 11, 2001. Jesuit priest James Martin believes that the images of rescue workers entering a sea of fire and smoke to save others—often at the expense of their own lives—showed us how God was present in the midst of this horrific suffering, offering up a modern-day parable for the world to see His love for what it truly is.

Americans became galvanized by this countercultural image of self-sacrifice that was so contrary to the contemporary self-absorbed and narcissistic gimme, gimme, gimme world at the time. Led by the example of firefighters who chose service over their own safety, the nation came together briefly immediately following the terrorist attacks on 9/11. Across the globe, people wanted to help in any way possible, from standing in line for hours to give blood to writing checks, crafting handmade toys for children who had just lost a parent, serving a cold bottle of water to workers at Ground Zero, and countless other acts of kindness. Even the children pitched in by doing what they could, writing letters and sending drawings and paintings to the firefighters.

United in our collective grief and bound together in fellowship, people of all faiths throughout the world practiced radical hospitality as we laid down our weapons and opened up our hearts. By being totally present, volunteers were able to respond to the needs of the rescue workers and those who lost loved ones without advancing their own religious and political agendas.

The fruit of the spirit metaphor came to life as clergy and laity joined forces, offering their talents for the good of the entire relief operation. Despite the fact that chaos ruled, U.S. citizens proved, for a few fleeting moments, that we were willing to implement the Greatest Commandment on a gigantic scale. I watched crowds of disparate individuals become the universal church right before my eyes. We put into practice the words of Swiss theologian Emil Brunner: "The Church exists by mission, just as a fire exists by burning. Where there is no mission, there is no church." And boy did we have a mission.

For the first time in my life, I thought I caught a glimpse of heaven here on earth. I saw the church operating horizontally, as laity and clergy worked side by side, each contributing their individual talents toward a common goal. Private and public expressions of faith fused together as people worked to feed the hungry, offer water to the thirsty, and welcome the stranger into their midst. Even as I reflect on this over four years later, I still get chills down my spine—my volunteer experience at the site was that moving and life-changing.

During the National Day of Prayer and Remembrance held on September 14, 2001, believers of all backgrounds gathered at prayer services in cathedrals, synagogues, mosques, churches, and other houses of worship around the world. We joined together as one collective family guided by the presence of God. Billy Graham prayed with the crowd that gathered at Washington's National Cathedral to reaffirm our conviction that "God cares for us whatever our ethnic, religious, or political background may be." Simply put, we are all God's children and must be treated as such.

On that same day, Sojourners, a Christian ministry whose mission is to proclaim and practice the biblical call to integrate spiritual renewal and social justice, echoed Graham's call for tolerance by joining forces with more than four thousand evangelical, Roman Catholic, Orthodox, and Protestant Christians to issue "Deny Them Their Victory: A Religious Response to Terrorism." This document states that we can prevent the terrorists from winning by refusing to submit to a world in their image. "We assert the vision of community, tolerance, compassion, justice, and the sacredness of human life, which lies at the heart of all our religious traditions."

Our esteemed president called for this National Day of Prayer, then stood with leaders of various Muslim groups and said, "The face of terror is not the truth faith of Islam. . . . Islam is peace. These terrorists don't represent peace. They represent evil and war. When we think of Islam, we think of a faith that brings comfort to a billion people around the world." Hard to believe that the same administration that invited representatives of fifty-three Muslim nations to the White House in November 2001 for a dinner marking the breaking of the daily fast during Ramadan would later turn a blind eye as Muslim prisoners had their basic human and religious rights violated en masse at Abu Ghraib and Guantánamo Bay.

But then again, the image of Bush extending an olive branch to heads of non-Christian nations does not jibe with the image of him atop the World Trade Center rubble on September 14, 2001, with bullhorn in hand, proclaiming, "I can hear you. The rest of the world hears you. And the people who knocked down these buildings will hear all of us soon." This good ol' boy was getting eager to instigate some Old Testament heinie-kicking.

> We are a nation that is unenlightened because of religion. I do believe that. I think that religion stops people from thinking. I think it justifies crazies. I think flying planes into a building was a faith-based initiative. I think religion is a neurological disorder.
>
> —Bill Maher, on MSNBC's *Scarborough Country*

In its position paper "For the Health of the Nation," the National Association of Evangelicals (NAE) urges governments "to pursue thoroughly nonviolent paths to peace before resorting to military force." Granted, this document wasn't adopted until October 7, 2004. But still, I have to wonder if Bush ever bothered to consult with his buddies at the NAE before he grabbed the bull-horn. Methinks they might have been able to offer some peaceful points for him to ponder. As expected, Congress got in the game, with both Democrats and Republicans gathering on the Capitol steps to sing "God Bless America." However, this patriotic tune was soon replaced by the battle hymn "Onward Christian Soldiers" as a bipartisan Congress initially supported the Bush administration's plans to invade both Afghanistan and Iraq.

> We know who the homicidal maniacs are. They are the ones cheering and dancing right now. We should invade their countries, kill their leaders and convert them to Christianity.
>
> —Ann Coulter, "This Is War"

On September 23, 2001, Yankee Stadium played ball by hosting "A Prayer for America," an interfaith service for the families and colleagues of the victims of the World Trade Center tragedy. A diverse range of religious and political leaders— including New York City Mayor Rudy Giuliani; New York Governor George Pataki; Edward Cardinal Egan; Rabbi Joseph Potasnik, a chaplain for the Fire Department of New York (FDNY); Imam Izak-El M. Pasha, a New York Police Department (NYPD) chaplain; and of course America's favorite religious guru, Oprah—joined forces in prayer and solidarity. Later, David Benke, president of Concordia Theological Seminary, caught holy hell from the Lutheran Church Missouri Synod for praying with heathens and other unholy heretics. In the eyes of some religious leaders, being right and righteous took priority over extending Jesus' love to their neighbors, comforting those in need, and all that pastoral jazz.

Almost as quickly as the towers came down, Jerry Falwell and Pat Robertson issued their own statements of sorts, blaming 9/11 in large part on the American Civil Liberties Union, abortionists, pagans, feminists, gays and lesbians, and the People for the American Way. A poll released on September 19, 2001, by the Pew Research Center for the People and the Press found that 69 percent of Americans reported they were praying more in the wake of the 9/11 attacks, though the poll failed to ask how many of these Americans were praying that just this once the Religious Right would let Jesus do the talking. While Jerry later quasi-apologized for playing this blame game, his doting disciples had already done considerable damage in the name of "Jerry's Jesus."

As President Bush continued to preach the message of revenge, news stories abounded about the violence committed against U.S. citizens who just happened to be Muslim. The USA PATRIOT Act of 2001 states, "Arab Americans, Muslim Americans, and Americans from South Asia play a vital role in our Nation and are entitled to nothing less than the full rights of every American."

However, a yearlong study conducted by the Domestic Human Rights Program of Amnesty International USA found that the unlawful use of race in police, immigration, and airport security procedures expanded since the terrorist attacks of September 11, 2001. Comments made by prominent evangelists like Jerry Vines, the former head of the Southern Baptist Convention, labeling Muhammad a "demon-possessed pedophile" and Franklin Graham calling Islam "an evil and wicked religion" only added to the inferno.

Regardless of W's personal feelings about the Muslim community, the United States marched off to war with the support of the president and both houses of Congress. Meanwhile, many religious leaders throughout the world were asking if we could maybe, you know, pray for some kind of guidance from the Almighty before entering into what could be another Vietnam-type scenario. During that time, the presence of the National Guard armed with AK-47s scattered throughout New York City and other major cities served as a stark reminder of the type of armed security that many countries throughout the world face on a daily basis.

Prayer stations sprang up all over the World Trade Center site as patriotic proselytizers and snake-oil salesmen swarmed around

Ground Zero. These self-appointed prophets apparently felt it was their God-given mission to "save the soul of Christian America." Some religious offenders, like the Scientology volunteer ministers in their caution-yellow jackets, were no longer seen around the site within a few weeks once it became clear that they were trying to recruit followers under the guise of providing mental health services.

Unfortunately, other individuals and groups were able to slip under the radar by pretending to represent an "official" religion. These self-anointed prophets would try to convert everyone around the site to their version of Christianity as they prayed to anyone with earshot that hopefully those who died on 9/11 without knowing Jesus were able to accept Him as their Lord and Savior before they drew their last breath. Meanwhile, the majority of the firefighters and police officers they were trying to convert were already baptized Christians, albeit of the Roman Catholic variety, who often just wanted to be left alone so they could grieve together in privacy. Simply put, these men were already putting their faith into practice by alternating their time between attending a countless stream of FDNY or NYPD funerals and digging for their brothers' bodies, as well as recovering civilian remains.

The pamphlets scattered throughout the site by these zealots ranged from insipid mainline drivel that possesses all the spiritual strength of smelling salts to the "God Loves America Best" jingoistic fare to the outright offensive *Why?* pamphlet, which proclaimed that 9/11 was a wake-up call for everyone to get right with Jesus. This Falwell-like rant, complete with a picture of the burning towers, was left on the tables for the firefighters to sample as they ate their meals. My award, though, for the most offensive Christian literature on display has to go to *The Day the Terrorists Struck!*—believe it or not, a children's book that reminds us all that while Satan was lurking in that big cloud of smoke as the Twin Towers burned, Jesus was riding high in the sky. Those who were not privileged to visit the site in person could view these same prayerful and patriotic messages compliments of the Internet and the Fox News Channel.

Of all the somewhat dubious material still on display, the product that I cannot view without holding my nose was *The Little Chapel That Stood,* a children's book that reminds our nation's already traumatized youth that "Ground Zero smoldered dark and grim. Our hearts stood still, then we pitched in." At first, I thought this book was a twisted *Lampoon*-esque parody until I realized that the actual author was a child psychologist.

Underneath the rubble of glitzy post-9/11 holier-than-thou memorabilia, I found a diamond in the rough when I picked up James Martin's poignant book *Searching for God at Ground Zero,* one of the few genuinely spiritual accounts of what transpired at the site. Another inspirational gem was Diana Butler Bass's book *Broken We Kneel: Reflections on Faith and Citizenship,* a series of reflections that helped me explore what it meant for me to be a Christian and an American in a post-9/11 world.

While there's definitely a need for religious guidance in the aftermath of an event of this magnitude that resulted from religious fanaticism, there's a fine line between instructive teaching and gratuitous self-promotion. The plethora of museum-quality videos and books, jewelry, posters, audiocassettes, and other religious memorabilia available for purchase proved that at some point, people forgot the teachings of John 7:18 and sought their own glory rather than glorifying Christ through their works.

This mass and at times crass merchandising by 9/11 ministries, which praised the dust and their deeds even before the debris had been cleared, reminded me of Jesus' commands in Matthew 6:1–4, in which the disciples are told to do their deeds in secret without sounding the trumpets. Some grassroots groups that formed after 9/11, such as ArtAID, contribute the proceeds from the sale of their artwork to support the ongoing needs of the 9/11 civilian and rescue worker community, as well as to provide healing art for those affected by other attacks such as the July 7, 2005, terrorist bombings in London and creating pieces to comfort the soldiers in Iraq. In contrast to the genuine nonprofit approach of ArtAID, little, if any, money raised from the sale of much of the 9/11-themed wares goes to support 9/11 ministries. Meanwhile, many of the rescue workers are now facing a multitude of physical and mental problems, with any remaining 9/11 funding dissipating rapidly.

Believe it or not, this mass-marketing of the church's ministry during disasters continues to this day. There are still a few religious folks who continue to circle the globe retelling the story of their heroics during the 9/11 recovery efforts as they try to drum up support for whatever book, CD, DVD, or other self-promotional product they're selling.

Yes, we will never forget 9/11, and we will always in our own ways memorialize that event and the lives lost on that day, but can we declare a moratorium on making 9/11 memorable, manageable, and marketable? While we're at it, can we put an end to the quasi-religious groups suggesting that the World Trade Center site needs to include such amenities as a New Age-y 9/11 healing garden or a politically correct but historically inaccurate homage to global terrorism? These proposals may be well intentioned, but the thing itself will end up looking silly at best. For those who want to contribute in a meaningful way, contact the people at ArtAID—they can clue you in on how to make a truly helpful contribution to the post-9/11 healing process.

Throughout the recovery effort, while I received praise from conservative churchgoers for being a "good American" by helping out, at times certain radical PC Christians (you know the ones that protest and party courtesy of their trust funds and tend to be supporters of the above-mentioned nefarious nonsense) chastised me for feeding conservative (read "right-wing Republican") firefighters and police officers. According to these pseudoprophets, there are more important social justice issues, such as protesting against the demonic White House, that should have demanded my attention instead.

I admit I have a very myopic view of the aftermath of 9/11, as my ministerial focus was on attending to the needs of the rescue workers. Frankly, I didn't learn until after the recovery effort had ended the full extent of interfaith seminars, protests, gatherings, and the like that focused on the Bush administration's decision to invade

Afghanistan and its treatment of American citizens who happened to be of the same hue as the 9/11 terrorists. But to assert that protesting is the best "Christian" response to 9/11 is simply ludicrous—we all need to pray and then let our individual conscience dictate where we should invest our energies. And for me, when I volunteered at the site, I felt a genuine connection with the rescue workers. We saw each other as fellow members of the body of Christ, and this relationship enabled us to transcend partisan politics.

I was where I felt I was called to be, though I tried to keep 9/11 from consuming my entire life. For too many people, Ground Zero became their Holy Grail, and they would do anything (and I mean *anything*) for a peek at the new Holy Land. The constant barrage of microphones in search of a quotable sound bite became an enticing temptation to a select number of religious leaders and 9/11 volunteers. Methinks that when Jesus said, "Let your light shine before men, that they may see your good works, and give glory to your Father in heaven" (Matthew 5:16), He wasn't referring to the glare of the media spotlight.

> Of all bad men, religious bad men are the worst.
> —C. S. Lewis, *Reflection on the Psalms*

Fortunately, the children around the world remained nonpartisan, and their heartfelt letters written in crayon and signed with X's and O's reminded us all why Jesus chose to surround Himself with little ones. They get the Gospel in its purest form, before we adults take over and try to intellectualize and justify the Bible to death.

The dichotomy between Christ's teachings and what I observed at the site only deepened as the months progressed. Many of us continued to serve in silence, knowing that the smiles and thank-yous we received from the rescue workers were enough of a reward in and of themselves. However, the never-ending quest for turf prevented a sitewide community from ever taking shape. While I saw the potential to redefine church when volunteers and rescue workers of different faiths and varying egos came together for Catholic Masses at the Ground Zero cross, little did we know that once the site closed, the cross would be copyrighted, with its likeness being used for both charitable and profit-making endeavors.

Since my father was an Episcopal priest, nothing should faze me when it comes to bad clergy behavior, but the rumors I heard about priestly posturing sickened my soul. Throughout the recovery effort, volunteers would hear graphic accounts of clergy throwing hissy fits over whose turn it was to bless the body bags and other examples of unpastoral behavior. As a journalist, I've covered a few post-9/11 events geared toward religious leaders, and unfortunately, this ungodly behavior is still evident. Meanwhile, the most touching stories—such as that of a small group of nuns quietly circling the pit as they tended to the rescue workers' everyday needs—all too often went unheard in the cacophony. But it was through the small but significant acts, such as an unknown chaplain saying a silent prayer, a volunteer pouring a cup of coffee, or a musician offering a song to accompany a meal, that Christ showed that He was still in our midst.

Paul's letters demonstrate that the early church had its share of egos and fights, so I guess all this infighting for spiritual supremacy is to be expected. I admit we all made some honest mistakes, and I know I made a few comments under stress that I wish I could take back. As a volunteer, I was not privy to the intricate details of what was really going on within the 9/11 inner spiritual circle, though I did get the strong sense that 9/11 church politics as played out at Ground Zero was akin to sampling street fair food. While it may look really enticing from a distance, it can give you quite the tummy ache if you're not careful. Add to the mix the international media attention of an event like 9/11, and it's enough to make any ego inflate.

Through my work with the 9/11 Advocates for a Fallen Heroes Memorial, I learned that what the firefighters really needed were not respite trips, more quilts, and homemade cookies; they wanted their colleagues to be grouped together and recognized as heroic soldiers who lost their lives while committing the most successful rescue operation in U.S. history. Likewise the civilians wish to have their loved ones remembered as more than random names on a wall. But as we debate how best to memorialize those we lost on 9/11, we have already buried more civilians and soldiers from the wars in Afghanistan and Iraq than were lost on that day. As of November 24, 2005, there had been 2,306 coalition troop deaths. Add to this count at least 15,568 U.S. troops that have been wounded in action, according to the Pentagon, not to mention the countless Afghani and Iraqi civilians killed, injured, or otherwise affected by the war. The numbers are mind-boggling, and I shudder to think how high these stats will be by the time you read this chapter.

Hallelujah Halliburton!

As soon as Bush declared war on Iraq on March 20, 2003, millions of antiwar activists staged rallies around the world, thus making it crystal-clear that the United States was no longer seen as a grieving country that needed support and succor. Instead, this good ol' boy country had been transformed into a superpower bad ass that needed a global smack upside the head. Here in the United States, the rallies were large in number, though sometimes the speakers spent more time decrying Bush's very existence and expressing overall disgust with his administration rather than stating a clear antiwar message.

Even some of the religious leaders who signed the document "What We're Fighting For: A Letter from America" in support of invading Afghanistan went "Whoa, wait a minute" when the Bush machine plowed into Iraq waving the Star-Spangled Banner emblazoned with the Halliburton logo. Pope John Paul II even quit praying over the pedophile priest fiasco long enough to say that the future depended partly on the earth's people and their leadership having the courage to say no to war. Quoting again from the NAE position paper "For the Health of the Nation": "We believe that if governments are going to use military force, they must use it in the service of peace and not merely in their national interest. Military force must be guided by the classic just war principles, which are designed to restrain violence by establishing the right conditions and the right conduct for fighting a war."

Bush appears to have blown off the both the pope and the NAE, as evidenced by his screw-the-UN, yee-haw-cowboy, go-git-'em attitude. Now, being a good evangelical, I can see on some level why he might "ignore" the pope, but why would he continue to disregard the proclamations of a major evangelical association? Once again, this makes me wonder if W is taking a "working vacation" of sorts during his weekly meetings with NAE president Ted Haggard.

The president these days seems to be led more by the teachings of Falwell, who proclaimed to Wolf Blitzer on CNN as late as October 24, 2004, that "you've got to kill the terrorists before the killing stops. And I'm for the president to chase them all over the world. If it takes ten years, blow them all away in the name of the Lord." I just reread the Gospels, and I can't find anything about Jesus giving the thumbs-up to blowing people to bits.

Now I could be wrong here when it comes to this concept of Jesus as a red-blooded machismo ass-kicker. I mean the NRA kicks off its annual convention with a "sportsmen's prayer breakfast" where, I assume, these prayer warriors prayerfully discern the best way to blast Bambi. (Sorry, bud, but advocating for semiautomatic weapons and promoting responsible hunting practices don't sit too well in my book.) Now, while everyone knows that former NRA president Charlton "Moses" Heston was one helluva pistol-packing prophet, I guess some folks who read the Bible a bit more literally than I do have come to the conclusion that their Lord and Savior should arm himself with an AK-47 or a TEC-9. But I digress.

Serving Those Who Serve

Fortunately, unlike Vietnam War veterans who returned from active duty to face throngs of protesters treating them with ridicule and scorn, at least today's vets receive a modicum of respect from all but the most ardent antiwar activists. In particular, the outreach efforts from the FDNY and 9/11 family communities to comfort the disabled soldiers and assist the families who lost a loved one in Afghanistan or Iraq bring tears to my eyes. Also, the FDNY sent

George W. Bush's Random Reflections on War and Peace, as Duly Reported by the White House Office of the Press Secretary

- "They used to put out there in the old west, a wanted poster. It said: 'Wanted, Dead or Alive.' " (Uttered to employees at the Pentagon, September 17, 2001)

- "Every nation, in every region, now has a decision to make. Either you are with us, or you are with the terrorists." (Spoken before a televised joint session of Congress, September 19, 2001)

- "I just want you to know that when we talk about war, we're really talking about peace." (Spoken while commemorating National Homeownership Month at the Department of Housing and Urban Development, June 18, 2002)

- "More Muslims have died at the hands of killers than—I say more Muslims—a lot of Muslims have died—I don't know the exact count—at Istanbul. Look at these different places around the world where there's been tremendous death and destruction because killers kill." (Stated during an interview with Mouafac Harb of the Middle East Television Network, January 29, 2004)

- "Nobody wants to be the 'war President.' I want to be the 'peace President.' " (Remark made at an Ask the President Event held at Kirkwood Community College in Cedar Rapids, Iowa, July 20, 2004)

- "Our enemies are innovative and resourceful, and so are we. They never stop thinking about new ways to harm our country and our people, and neither do we." (Stated at the signing of H.R. 4613, the Defense Appropriations Act for Fiscal Year 2005, August 5, 2004)

- "In this different kind of war, we may never sit down at a peace table. But make no mistake about it, we are winning, and we will win." (Spoken at the Eighty-Sixth Annual Convention of the American Legion, August 31, 2004)

- "Free societies are hopeful societies. And free societies will be allies against these hateful few who have no conscience, who kill at the whim of a hat—at the drop of a hat." (Remarks made during the Victory 2004 Luncheon, September 17, 2004)

(continued)

- "But Iraq has—have got people there that are willing to kill, and they're hard-nosed killers. And we will work with the Iraqis to secure their future." (Stated during a White House press conference, April 28, 2005)

- "One of the main jobs we have here in Washington is to protect our country. You see, not only did the attacks help accelerate a recession, the attacks reminded us that we are at war." (Observations made while giving a speech to a meeting of builders and contractors at the Capital Hilton, June 8, 2005)

- "We will not yield to these people, will not yield to the terrorists. We will find them, we will bring them to justice, and at the same time, we will spread an ideology of hope and compassion that will overwhelm their ideology of hate." (Offering condolences to the people of London, July 7, 2005)

- "We are finding terrorists and bringing them to justice. We are gathering information about where the terrorists may be hiding. We are trying to disrupt their plots and plans. Anything we do to that effort, to that end, in this effort, any activity we conduct, is within the law. We do not torture." (Spoken during a press conference in Panama City while meeting with President Torrijos of Panama, November 7, 2005)

equipment to their brother firefighters trying to protect the war-torn city of Kabul; other programs provide similar services. In addition, some groups formed in the aftermath of 9/11 continue to reach out to help victims of other disasters, including the Oklahoma City bombings, the tsunami disaster, the 2005 terrorist attack in London, and the devastation in the Gulf Coast caused by Hurricanes Katrina and Rita.

So what are some of the ways in which Christians can support the troops even though they do not support the war? Right before Memorial Day 2005, *Sojourners* asked its readers to call on the United States to uphold its responsibilities to veterans, practice real compassion, and truly support the troops. The suggestion was for everyone to send a letter to the editor of the local newspaper to help raise awareness of veterans' issues. Even churches that are divided over whether one should wear a red, white, and blue flag pin or an antiwar black armband to church can come to a consensus that just as Jesus took care of those in need, we need to be there for soldiers and their families.

Rather than debate the theological reasons why this is an unjust war, I think Jesus would cut through the crap and, well, just be Himself. He'd be out in the field consoling the mother who just buried her soldier son, being the arms for the disabled sergeant who can no longer hug her children, or delivering a bag of groceries to an active-duty soldier's family who cannot make ends meet on a reservist's paycheck. In addition to supporting these heroes, it's a pretty safe bet that Jesus' heart would also be with Church World Service, the Salvation Army, and other religious organizations that have provided practical assistance by delivering much needed medical supplies, food, water, and other necessities to civilians suffering in Afghanistan and Iraq.

Speaking of spreading Christ's message of universal love, for many individuals throughout the world, September 11, 2001, represented one of those singular moments in history when religious communities became unfrozen and new possibilities for community were able to emerge. Every time a group of us serves in a Salvation Army canteen at a fire, FDNY or NYPD funeral, disaster drill, or some other event, I feel that we are able to somehow respond to the firefighters and police officers in the spirit of radical hospitality that was started at 9/11.

Looking for the Light

Unfortunately, the individual churches by and large appear to have closed their doors to the needs of rescue workers they ministered to during the recovery operation, even though these people continue to come to the aid of the city. Except for a telling memorial to the rescue workers at Saint Joseph's Chapel in Battery Park City and some other local memorials and outreach efforts at mostly Catholic parishes, New York City churches have remained largely silent when it comes to assisting these everyday heroes with their ongoing needs and concerns.

The question remains how leaders of faith communities can harness the collective spirit that emerged during the recovery effort and invest it in future ministries. While the church truly came alive as the universal church during the recovery effort, it feels as though too many churches have returned to "normal" as though nothing transformative happened during those eight and a half months. Even though the terrorist attacks on 9/11 were fueled at least in part by religious fanaticism, it's the laity, not the clergy, who are taking the lead in defining what constitutes sacred space at a site that for many has now become hallowed ground.

Think for a moment what New York City and the world would be like if we could all follow the example of the firefighters who on 9/11 chose self-sacrifice over self-interest and in so doing performed the most successful rescue operation in U.S. history by leading more than twenty-five thousand people to safety.

I know this is all starting to sound bit Hallmark-y, but Jesus did say that no one has greater love than this, to lay down one's life for one's friends (see John 15:13). And in today's cynical *Who Wants to Be a Millionaire?* world, as Americans frolic on *Temptation Island* in their quest to be the ultimate *Survivor*, there are those individuals, like the firefighters, police officers, and soldiers, who still put His teachings into practice. Praise be to God.

An Interview with Yale Theology Professor Miroslav Volf

Excerpted from *The Wittenburg Door*, January-February 1999

DOOR: Can one forgive those who have perpetrated particularly heinous crimes?

VOLF: The answer is simple, "I must forgive." And if I cannot, I must be liberated from my inability to want to forgive and from my inability to actually do the forgiving that I may want to do. Forgiveness can be learned. As my former teacher and friend Lew Smedes—Mr. Forgiveness, you can almost call him—has argued in many of his books, forgiveness is an art. It will help us master the art if we keep in mind that we all are sinners, not all equal sinners but all equally sinners. The world cannot be neatly divided into innocent victims and guilty perpetrators. There were periods in history when Croats were on the whole not victims in relation to the Serbs but perpetrators; and during the most recent war not a few Croats acted as victim-turned-into-perpetrator in search for revenge. So we Croats will find it easier to forgive if we realize that we ourselves desperately need forgiveness.

DOOR: Isn't there a danger that turning the other cheek could lead to violence and oppression?

VOLF: Sure there is such a danger. There is even a danger that the one who turns the other cheek will lose the head on which the cheek sits! But does this danger justify hitting the cheek of the one who has hit our cheek? Will the exchange of blows lead to peace and justice? I very much doubt that. And if it did, that peace would in fact be violence portraying itself as peace, and that justice would in fact be oppression parading as justice. It is important to underscore that Christians do not turn the other cheek because this is the most effective way to combat violence and oppression. If this were the case, once the effectiveness of this strategy no longer obtained, they could switch from commitment to nonviolence to engagement in violence. So what then if turning the other cheek proves ineffective? The best response I know—a response that merits careful pondering—is the one given by the late John Howard Yoder: "The relationship between the obedience of God's people and the triumph of God's cause is not a relationship of cause and effect but one of cross and resurrection."

DOOR: How does exclusion bring about evils such as the atrocities committed in your homeland?

VOLF: Ethnic cleansing, which was pursued with such brutal force in the former Yugoslavia, is one particularly deadly form of exclusion. The practice of exclusion operates with a logic of purity:

(continued)

the blood must be pure, the territories must be pure, the origin must be pure, and the goal must be pure. Whatever muddles the purity must be removed. We want a pure world and we push "others" out of it; we want to be pure ourselves and we eject "otherness" from within ourselves.

DOOR: Why do you see exclusion as a sin?

VOLF: Because the ultimate goal of human life is a community of love in the embrace of the Triune God. Any action or institution that seeks to eliminate, assimilate, and dominate or simply abandon the other—any exclusionary practice—is sinful; it transgresses against the goal for which God has created humanity and therefore against the will of God. Because Christians believe that God is love, they must believe that exclusion is a fundamental sin.

DOOR: How did Jesus' earthly ministry address the issue of exclusion?

VOLF: If I read the Gospels rightly, Jesus pursued a dual strategy of renaming the behavior that was falsely labeled sinful and remaking the people who have actually sinned or have suffered misfortune. The strategy of renaming what was falsely labeled "sinful" or "unclean" is aimed at abolishing the warped system of exclusion in the name of an order that God has made "clean" and pronounced "good." The strategy of remaking sinful people aimed at tearing down the barriers created by wrongdoing in the name of God whose love knows no boundaries. By this double strategy Jesus condemned the world of exclusion—a world in which the innocent are labeled evil and driven out and a world in which the guilty are not sought out and brought into the communion.

3

CHRISTIAN HOSPITALITY, RNC STYLE

> The whole modern world has divided itself into Conservatives
> and Progressives. The business of Progressives is to go on
> making mistakes. The business of the Conservatives is to
> prevent the mistakes from being corrected.
> —*G. K. Chesterton, 1924*

During the 2004 Republican National Convention held in New York
City, I decided to become as a fly on the wall—a journalist in search
of the "political" Jesus. Fortunately, I am duly credentialed for such a
dubious task. I had on my person not only my color-coded and num-
bered Republican National Committee (RNC) press pass but also
my voter registration card listing my party affiliation as an "independent," as well as both my baptismal and confirmation certificates.

When I entered the RNC press office to obtain a listing of the
hospitality suites for the American Family Association, Focus on
the Family, Family Research Council, Christian Coalition, and
other like-minded souls, I was greeted with one of those "Jesus may
love you, but please just get your sorry ass the hell out of here" frozen
smiles. When I asked why most of the Religious Right were not in
public view during this week's festivities, I got the clear sense that
my quest for truth-telling just sent the U.S. Department of Homeland Security advisory system into a tailspin.

Those few conservative leaders who would speak to the media
(Phyllis Schlafly—you go, girl!) claimed that if I proved to be oh-
so-holy, I could find Jesus down on the convention floor at Madison
Square Garden all decked out in red, white, and blue. Even though

Ralph Reed & Co. pulled no-shows during the convention, the National Federation of Republican Assemblies (NFRA) came to the rescue of the righteous by offering food, fellowship, and fundamentalism. (Note: That's the NFRA, which is not to be confused with the NRA—the former is for God, and the latter is for guns.)

The all-American "official" RNC press briefings at Madison Square Garden proved that the hypnotic charm of political genius Karl Rove was working at full tilt. Clearly, the party bigwigs put something into the coffee that turned everyone into fawning sycophants.

Even though the Republicans scrapped a planned trip to Ground Zero for fear they would be seen as "opportunistic," well-worn World War II slogans and other jingoistic fare were greeted with patriotic salutes and thunderous applause. The faithful were told to remember September 11, 2001, and the first thing the entire United States felt on that day, the most American feeling of all—*patriotism*. Every reason to vote for GWB was in there somewhere—a God-fearing America replete with morals and values and a place for the unborn child—a Safer World, a More Hopeful America.

The crowd kept clapping and barking in unison like well-choreographed, trained baby seals still naive enough to believe that their wildlife habitats will be preserved. Karl Rove proved his worth in political gold by convincing all the major players and the mainstream media that King George W. was the rightful ruler. He pulled off this sleight of hand despite the fact that not only was this particular emperor wearing no clothes, but also that if elected, the Bush administration's draconian policies would make the rest of us run around buck nekkid as well.

As expected, phrases like "interfaith dialogue," "congressional approval," "Kyoto Protocol," and "International Criminal Court" were notably missing from these PAX TV (now *i*TV)–type salutes. Truly, God had blessed the Republican Party for standing up to the Middle Eastern infidels.

One of the few pro-life speakers permitted on the podium, Senator Elizabeth Dole, used her nonprime speaking slot to connect the dots between following Christ and voting Republican: "Two thousand years ago, a man said, 'I have come to give life and to give it in full.' In America, I have the freedom to call that man Lord, and I do. . . . The right to worship God isn't something Republicans invented, but it is something Republicans will defend."

Libby and other speakers reminded the fundamental faithful to be wary of liberals. Just think what a better world it would be if we all—the whole world—joined the Presidential Prayer Team and chanted "Four more years!" Or if all politicians really acted like there was no separation of church and state, and we all learned how to be a servant-leader just like Bush.

As the cheering crowd bowed before Bush, thus anointing him to serve for another four-year reign, the words of Matthew 7:15 telling me to beware of false prophets rang in my ears until my brain hurt. The president articulated his strongly held religious convictions, offering the consolation that at least you knew where he stood on the issues. Dubya reminded his devout fans that if he could take his personal ideals and extrapolate them into social policy and then apply this to the American family, the U.S. government, and the entire world, everything would become right and religious and Republican.

Protest 'n' Party

During this RNC circus, there was plenty of action on the liberal front. Whenever I had some free time, I tried observe how those more progressive Christians, who preach tolerance from the pulpit, were actually responding to their perceived religious enemies in their midst.

Throughout Manhattan, select progressive churches joined forces with what I swear had to be a legitimate agency, the No-RNC Clearinghouse, an unofficial Web site designed to serve as a resource databank for the hordes of protesters that descended on the city during the Republican National Convention. These churches offered services and support for those people who flocked to the Big Apple to express their dissent and profound disagreement with the policies of the current administration. They publicized their willingness to coordinate activities ranging from healing and feeding stations to legal and voting information, training sessions, film screenings, live performances, and motivational speakers.

Several churches that housed the activists went so far as to display anti-Bush materials that proclaimed an intense dislike of all things Republican. (What's a nice church like you doing with paraphernalia offering a rather graphic description of what Bush and Cheney could do with their respective body parts?) As the week progressed, I found myself questioning why any church that professed to follow the teachings of Christ would allow such hateful material to be displayed.

As I approached these happenings, gatherings, and be-ins, the sounds of Dylan and the Doors that permeated these "spiritual" respite centers transported me back to my childhood days protesting against the Vietnam War with my father and other like-minded leftist priests and professors. I knew from past protest experiences that if I presented myself as a tie-dyed hardcore protester professing my undying allegiance to the Democratic Party, I would be greeted with open arms and invited to join in the barbeque and beer parties. However, since I dressed in nondescript black to present myself as a nonpartisan journalist, I was often viewed as not a potential comrade but a possible enemy, someone who must be avoided at all costs.

The lyrics to "Easy to Be Hard," that classic anthem from the '60s-era rock musical *Hair*, replayed in my head as I met Christians who repeatedly sounded the call for social justice. However, despite their alleged peaceful proclamations, these activists demonstrated overt hostility toward the perceived Republican enemy and feigned indifference toward people like me because they couldn't quite decipher our particular political leanings. Even though I am a prenatal Episcopalian (my dad was an Episcopal priest—you do the science), for the first time in my life, I did not feel that I belonged in any of these "Christian" houses of worship—not even those sporting red, white, and blue signs proclaiming "The Episcopal Church Welcomes You."

The christian coalition Presidential Prayer Primer

This prayer primer was first published in *The Wittenburg Door* in May-June 1995, after the Republicans took control of Congress in 1994. The prayers were updated after the 2004 election.

Prayers of Self-Praise and Adoration

Glory be to me on high, and on earth, assault weapons and family values imposed upon all men. I praise me, I bless me, I worship me, I glorify me, I give thanks to me for my great glory. Amen. Glory be to the Pat, and to his Holy Coalition; as it should have been in the beginning, is now and must be until we are raptured away. Amen.

A Prayer for When a Republican Candidate Is Tempted

Lord and Master, Pat Robertson, who thyself wast tempted as I am, yet appeareth to be without sin, give me thy wisdom to partake of my temptations without suspicion. Enable me to engage in all evil thoughts and passions, obtain all political entitlements, and to learn, like thee, how to appear holy and righteous, thus blaming all my sins on the Democrats. Amen.

A Prayer for Widows, Orphans, and the Homeless and Those Who Minister to Them

Praise the Lord. Amen.

A Prayer for the Elimination of Our Undemocratic Enemies

O Pat, the Ruler of all, whose CBN ministry commands us to seek the annihilation of all nonbelievers: Lead all democratically elected world leaders to accept Jesus Christ as their Lord and Savior, so that we can stand before you in a New World Order united as one body of godly male leadership. Amen.

A Prayer in Thanksgiving for the 2004 Presidential Election

Almighty Council for National Policy, who dost give us money so that we can use all our power and privileges, guide us; we thank you for anointing George W. Bush to be our next selected president. We pray that by thy supreme guidance, he will appear a godly man, who will be enslaved by the will of thy Council for National Policy and can fulfill thy self-righteous purposes. In the name of our Lord and Savior Jesus Christ. Amen.

The Prayer of Saint Kerry of DNC

Lord, help me to flee from the liberals' woes. Where there are lies, let me stand still; where there are veterans, vacate; where there is change, chaos; where there is fear, flee; where there is scandal, silence; where there are values, vacuum; where there is foreplay, frown. Grant that I may not so much seek to be prophetic as to placate; to be presidential as to ponder; to chasten as to be chaste. For it is in retreating that I advance; it is in denial that I will deny; and it is in lying that I'll be elected as president. Amen.

While I am aware that some spiritually serious events were held, such as the "Mobilization 2004/Let Justice Roll: Faith and Community Voices Against Poverty" rally at the Riverside Church, much of what I observed veered more toward the silly side. My award for the most ridiculous ritual sponsored by a church during the Republican National Convention goes to A31, a grassroots activist organization dedicated to promoting "nonviolent civil disobedience and direct action." I was at Madison Square Garden watching Bush receive his nomination, so I didn't see this spectacle with my own eyes. But according to the material I read, it appears as though one of the most progressive churches in New York City joined forces with A31 (which, by the way, stands for August 31, the date of the event). The end result of this unholy union was a program titled "Drum Circle, Peace Ritual, & Totally Tyranny-Free Party for the People." According to the program flyer, "This happening called together Radical Faeries for an evening of peace and love-making ritual in opposition to the war-mongering Republican rally at MSG." You just can't make up this kinda stuff.

Despite the overabundance of "Have a Nice Day" pins, peace symbol necklaces, and peyote available for sale, dissent appeared to be raging among the different protest factions. The aging Deadheads stopped twiddling their love beads long enough to fight for flower-power supremacy with their younger vegan progressive counterparts. Some of the more hardened activists weren't taking too kindly to having their sacred turf invaded. While the text-message, high-speed Internet generation wanted to enact more innovative forms of protest against the establishment, the tie-dyed diehards wanted to, like, reenact the '60s, like, all over again, man. Guess they somehow forgot that Martin Luther King Jr. was but twenty-five when he became pastor of the Dexter Avenue Baptist Church in Montgomery, Alabama, and served as a member of the executive committee of the NAACP. Alas, history is riddled with accounts of the old guard refusing to relinquish the crown to the younger generation.

Yeah, this is all cutesy and fun, but in the words of William Shakespeare, the anti-Bush protests proved to be "full of sound and fury, signifying nothing." In particular, the faint cries of at least two million New Yorkers across the five boroughs who are at risk of going hungry every day got lost in the dissenters' displays of disgust with the polices of Rove-Cheney-Bush. Why did Democratic presidential candidate John Kerry and so many of the dissidents fail to lift up a positive alternative social agenda in response to their profound dislike of the Bush administration?

Throughout the week, I noticed that some self-proclaimed liberal clergy dared not even speak His name, even though Jesus made it pretty clear in the Beatitudes where He stood on issues of social justice. When Jesus warned His followers to be "wise as serpents and innocent as doves" (Matthew 10:16), that didn't mean Christians should remain passive. Jesus' point was that we should understand our opponents' tactics but not respond in an ungodly manner. And although He was speaking in terms of religious opposition, the concept easily transfers to the political arena. In any event, too many progressive clergy in New York City

> In your reelection, God has granted America—though she doesn't deserve it—a reprieve from the agenda of paganism. . . . Don't equivocate. Put your agenda on the front burner and let it boil. You owe the liberals nothing. They despise you because they despise your Christ.
> —Bob Jones III, former president of Bob Jones University, in a letter to George W. Bush following the November 2004 election

failed to acknowledge Jesus as the One who was the inspiration behind their social justice actions.

My experience that entire week was limited to activities for which I received an invitation, official events I could access via my RNC press pass, or gatherings I found out about through the No-RNC Clearinghouse. There may have been some meaningful religious exchanges that somehow slid under the radar. But after a week in Stepfordland, it became crystal clear to me that like Elvis, Jesus had left the building.

Thus ends my 2004 political convention coverage. I did not attend the Democratic National Convention because *The Wittenburg Door*'s measly budget wouldn't have covered the expense involved of traveling to another city. But I'm sure if I had been there, I would have had an equally ridiculous and spiritually bankrupt experience.

Democratic Doublespeak

"We worship an awesome God in the Blue States. . . . We are one people, all of us pledging allegiance to the Stars and Stripes, all of us defending the United States of America."

What strikes me as telling was the eloquence of Illinois Senator Barack Obama's words in his keynote address at the 2004 Democratic National Convention when juxtaposed against the vile images of protesters demonstrating during the convention. Seeing that the individuals voicing their objections to the DNC platform were corralled into detentionlike facilities, should we really believe that the Democrats envision a "unified" America?

The Democratic National Committee's Reinterpretation of the Ten Commandments

1. We are the Democratic National Committee, the DNC, who brought liberals out of the land of Clinton and into Kerryesque ruin. Liberals shall support no other committee but us.

2. Liberals shall not support any other candidate, whether in the form of anyone that votes Working Party, or that votes Green, or that is a member of another left-wing party. Liberals shall give money to us and support us; for we the DNC your party are a lapdog party, supporting Clinton throughout his transgressions, remaining a true and loyal political pawn. And the DNC will provide pork to the thousandth contributor of those who vote Democratic and keep funding our campaigns.

3. You shall not make jokes in the name of the DNC your party, for liberals have no sense of humor and cannot understand the punch lines.

4. Remember election day and vote Democratic. The rest of the year, you may do as you please. But election day is a holy day to the DNC your party; all liberals must vote Democratic, both you, your son or your daughter, your male and female employees, your pets, even the illegal nannies you employ.

5. For eight years, the DNC supported Hillary and Bill, the DNC and all that is Democratic and remained a loyal servant; we even blessed Gore and Kerry and endorsed them. Honor our slate of candidates, so that some day we may return to the White House and the DNC can reclaim our rightful inheritance.

6. You shall not issue any fatwas or inflict any forms of punishment, abuse or neglect on anyone who is deemed to be an enemy of the Democratic party without the prior consent of the DNC leadership.

7. You shall not accuse fellow Democrats of adultery.

8. You shall not question the sources of donations to the DNC.

9. You shall not bear false witness against your fellow Democrats.

10. You shall not vote for a Republican; you shall not support a Republican's bills, initiatives, amendments, or anything that is endorsed by a Republican.

4

HOW WOULD JESUS VOTE?

Two things made this country great: white men and
Christianity. . . . Every problem that has arisen can
be directly traced back to our departure from God's
law and the disenfranchisement of the white men.
—*Republican State Representative Don Davis, e-mailed
to every member of the North Carolina House and Senate*

Given that my last name ain't Falwell, Robertson, or LaHaye, I
can't claim to speak for Christ. But based on what I read in the
Gospels, when it comes to taking one's faith into the voting booth,
my hunch is that Jesus would tell the electorate to beware of false
prophets traipsing around the country decked out in sheep's clothing that disguises the fact that they're ravenous wolves (see
Matthew 7:15).

Frankly, I am not so sure how the Lord and Savior would feel
about today's houses of worship doubling as political battle stations. During the 2004 election, both conservative and liberal
churches carried out voter registration drives as a part of their "outreach ministry." However, neither political party seems to give a
hoot when it comes to reducing the root causes of poverty that force
people to take advantage of church-sponsored outreach programs
in the first place.

As a nonpartisan religious satirist, I confess that I have delighted
in lampooning the political antics of the Religious Right for years,
offering the 1994 Religious Rightly elected Congress "The Christian Coalition Presidential Prayer Primer" (*The Wittenburg Door,*

Advice from Dr. James Dobson

This piece was originally published in *The Wittenburg Door*, September-October 2004. Dr. Dobson is president of the nonprofit organization Focus on the Family, P.O. Box 444, Colorado Springs, CO 80903; http://www.family.org.

QUESTION: I need help understanding how to interpret my Iraqi prisoners' behavior. My problem is that I don't know how to react when they annoy me. I'm sure there are many minor infractions that a Christian world leader should just ignore. At other times, immediate discipline seems necessary. But I'm not sure I'll react in the right way on the spur of the moment.—W.

DR. DOBSON: Obviously, the first thing you have to do is determine the Iraqis' intent, their feelings, and their thoughts. Is there evidence that the Iraqis are challenging your authority? The more blatant their defiance, the more critical it is to respond with decisiveness.

When citizens of a Middle Eastern country scream obscenities at a Christian occupying power, they have moved into the realm of willful defiance. As the words imply, it is a deliberate act of disobedience that occurs when the internees know what the Americans want, but they clench their fists, dig in their heels, and prepare for battle. When this kind of nose-to-nose confrontation occurs between captured insurgents and their authority figures, your godly leadership is on the line.

For specific disciplining techniques, check out my book, *The New Dare to Discipline.*

QUESTION: Should I be punishing my strong-willed president for every little thing he does wrong? I'd be on his back every minute of the day.—Tim LaH.

DR. DOBSON: I am *not* suggesting that you be oppressive in dealing with everyday behavior. The issues that should get your attention are those that deal with respect for you as the primary "behind the scenes" operator of his presidency. When he is defiant, sassy, and disobedient, you should confidently and firmly step in and lead. After making it clear what is expected, and the president still refuses to obey, a mild slap on the hands while saying "no" will usually discourage repeat episodes. If the misbehavior continues, take away his Rold Gold pretzels for a time. My book *The Strong-Willed Child* is chock full of examples on how to curb his defiant behavior.

QUESTION: How can I acquaint my son with the need for responsible behavior throughout his life? He is desperately in need of this understanding.—Poppy

DR. DOBSON: One important objective during the pre-presidency period is to teach a child that actions have inevitable consequences. One of the most serious casualties in a permissive society is the failure to connect those two factors, behavior and consequences.

For instance, a child sleeps through all his classes, but his school makes allowances for his lineage and takes no action. All through childhood, his loving parents seem determined to intervene between behavior and consequences, breaking the connection and preventing the valuable learning that could and should have occurred. I hope my book *Bringing Up Boys* can bring you advice and encouragement during this difficult time. On the other hand, it's not like he went AWOL or anything.

QUESTION: Can you give us a guideline for how much work a president should be given to do?—Dick and Karl

DR. DOBSON: There should be a healthy balance between work and play. Many world leaders of the past had daily chores that made life pretty difficult. Early in the morning and again after work they would draft legislation, meet with world leaders, debate public policy, and go to boring summit meetings. Little time was left for fun, and world domination became a pretty drab experience. That was an extreme position, and I certainly don't favor its return. Contrast that workaday responsibility with liberals today that require nothing of their world leaders. Both extremes, as usual, are harmful to world leadership. Giving him an exposure to responsibility and work, but preserving time for play and fun can help him find the logical middle ground. I know this is a difficult balancing act, which is why I hope my book *Parenting Isn't for Cowards* will prove to be a valuable help here.

QUESTION: My husband has become increasingly lazy over the past couple of years. He lies around the White House and will sleep half a day on Saturday. He complains about being tired a lot. Is this typical of presidents? How should I deal with it?—Laura

(continued)

DR. DOBSON: It is not uncommon for world leaders to experience fatigue during their years in office. After a contentious election campaign, their mental resources are suddenly being invested in a rapid growth process, leaving less energy for other activities. This period doesn't last very long and is usually followed by the most energetic time of life.

I would suggest, first, that you schedule your husband for a routine physical examination to rule out the possibility of a more serious explanation for his fatigue. Your husband has turned almost overnight from a governor to a world leader. Some of the mental characteristics you are observing are part of the long-term transformation. Do everything you can to facilitate it. Additional pointers can be found in my book *Preparing for Adolescence: How to Survive the Coming Years of Change.*

May-June 1995; see Chapter Three) and serving as a scribe for Pat Robertson as he detailed his vision for taking Republicans to the Promised Land Armageddon-style in "The Revelation of Robertson" (*The Wittenburg Door*, September-October 1996). This piece was revised as "The Revelation of Dubya" and published in July-August 2001 issue of *The Wittenburg Door* after the Bushies selected George W. as the heir apparent (see Appendix A). Also, I became a vocal coach of sorts in helping George W. Bush articulate his religious views in "Bush Beliefs" (*The Wittenburg Door*, March-April 2001) and even did a bit of ghostwriting for James Dobson ("Advice from Dr. James Dobson," *The Wittenburg Door*, September-October 2004) to assist the Bush clan in carrying out their vision for an America that is right, religious, and Republican.

And while Kerry could never fill Clinton's comedic shoes, he possessed enough hemming, hawing, and hypocrisy that I figured I could definitely write a few a good old-fashioned Democratic slams should he get elected. Regardless of who won, it seemed that my career as a religious satirist would be secure for at least the next four years. However, given the lack of attention to issues such as outsourcing of jobs to India, the rising number of Americans without health care, and bipartisan waffling on the war in Iraq, there was no guarantee that we would have a secure, safe, and sane future regardless of who was in the White House.

I wasn't able to hitch a ride on Call to Renewal's six-state, eleven-city bus tour, but anyone who tries to drive home the message that poverty is a religious and moral election issue is all right by me. I do wonder, though, why Kerry & Co. didn't hear the roar of this Christian caravan until it rear-ended them a few times. I also wasn't able to fill up on grape juice and saltines on the Southern Baptist Convention's iVoteValues.com Mobile Voter Registration Rig and Information Center, though given the size of this 77-foot sucker, I doubt that "care for God's creation" was one of the values under consideration.

Even my favorite source of comedy material for eight cigar-smoke-filled years got into the act by endorsing "Mobilization 2004: Recovering America's Spiritual, Moral, and Democratic Values." In his sermonesque speech delivered at the Riverside Church in New York City the day before the Republican National Convention got under way, Bill Clinton reminded his party faithful that "religious values can include commitment to the common good, concern for the poor and vulnerable, the middle-class families, the preservation of our God-given environment, unity over division, and truth in campaign advertising." Nice talk. Let's see how this message stacked up, though, against the backdrop of his '96 family-values-saturated campaign. If I remember correctly, Dick Morris, Senator Jesse Helms's former campaign manager and a real bastion of moral virtue, orchestrated Clinton's reelection campaign. Don't ask, don't tell.

During Bill Moyers's turn at the Riverside Church's pulpit, the public television broadcaster and liberal icon reminded Americans to "recover the faith that takes on the corruption of power. A faith that challenges complacency at both parties. . . . Jesus drove the moneychangers from the Temple of Jerusalem. We must drive them from the temples of democracy." Hmmm—guess neither the Democrats nor the Republicans watch PBS much these days.

Leading by Example

In the Sermon on the Mount, Jesus makes it pretty clear that anyone who follows Him must first and foremost be an advocate for the poor and the meek and all that other good stuff He talked about in the Beatitudes. He never preached directly on topics such as creationism, homosexuality, school choice, or abortion, so I'm not so sure that these would be central issues in Jesus' campaign platform. Although Jesus would want a prince of peace and not a God of war, he'd agree with Moyers that the leader should be able to raise some hell and knock over the moneychangers' tables whenever the Temple gets too bloody corrupt.

While today's political leaders are obsessed with advancing their own agenda, Brian McLaren notes that Jesus didn't overturn the tables "so that all the wrongs could be excluded. No. Jesus turned the tables and scattered the doves and coins so that the temple could once again become a house of prayer *for all nations*—an inclusive place that welcomes *all* into the transforming mystery of prayer and worship, not only the 'already right' or the 'rich in spirit.' "

Unlike many of our contemporary leaders, Jesus seems to have this separation of church and state idea down pat, serving as a prophetic voice to proclaim the Word of God without being a pawn of the Roman government. That's a distinction made by Swiss theologian Karl Barth, one of the leading thinkers in the neo-orthodox movement, when he said preachers should preach with the Bible in one hand and the newspaper in the other. Some legitimate concerns were raised during the 2004 election about the DNC possibly tiptoeing along the fine line that separates church and state. But the RNC clearly drove a gas-guzzling eighteen-wheeler across the church-state line by bankrolling Web sites with derogatory names like http://www.kerrywrongforcatholics.com, http://www.kerrywrongformormons.com, and http://www.kerrywrongforevangelicals.com that were aimed directly at specific religious groups.

Speaking of the Religious Right, the story of the Pharisee and the tax collector in Luke 18:10–14 pretty clearly demonstrates that

Jesus isn't thrilled with leaders who talk up their holiness and strut around saying, "Lookit me—I be praying!" Try getting that lesson across to the organizers of the Presidential Prayer Breakfast, the Presidential Prayer Team, or *The 700 Club*'s latest Bless Bush and Damn the Democrats Prayathon; they'll probably Bible bless you till it hurts.

Jesus wants prayerful leaders, but as McLaren reminds us "Jesus came as a liberating, revolutionary leader, freeing us from the dehumanization and oppression that come from 'the powers that be' in our world (including religious powers). His kingdom, then, is a kingdom not of oppressive control but of dreamed-of freedom, not of coercive dominance but of liberating love, not of top-down domination but of bottom-up service, not of a clenched iron fist but of open, wounded hands extended in a welcoming embrace of kindness, gentleness, forgiveness, and grace."

Christ demonstrated what it means to be a servant-leader by washing the feet of His disciples (see John 13:5–16) during the last meal they would share together during His earthly ministry. Unfortunately, this story has been used in way too many Christian leadership seminars and stewardship trainings to the point that the power of this message can often get lost amid a slew of sanctified and sanitized PowerPoint presentations.

But Jesus, radical rule-breaker that He was, chose to break down conventional social barriers during His earthly ministry by cleansing lepers, socializing with the untouchables of His day, and performing other actions that no proper Jewish leader of the time would ever have done for fear of being labeled "unclean" and thus banished from the Temple. During His last meal on earth, rather than enlist a servant to clean their dusty feet so that Jesus and His disciples could partake of their meal properly, Jesus decided do the task Himself.

In performing this simple act, Jesus showed that while He may have been their leader, He was also a servant who wasn't afraid to get down 'n' dirty to demonstrate to His disciples that as a leader, He must be humble and willing to put others' needs ahead of His own status. David Buschman, Baptist chaplain at Princeton University (and if he's Baptist you know he's gotta be biblical) says this about the passage: "This was not merely a staged photo opportunity [or] a clever grandstanding scheme (see Matthew 6:1) [or] a community service project chosen for its résumé-enhancing capability. Rather, Jesus the Christ, who claimed to have all authority in heaven and on earth (see Matthew 28:18), was smart enough (in his head), free enough (in his heart), and willing enough (with his hands) to serve, to give, to yield."

Henri Nouwen, Catholic priest and noted author, observed that we have been tempted to replace this self-sacrificial love with power. He reflects on the lure and seemingly irresistible temptation to substitute power for the admittedly hard task of loving others. "It seems easier to be God than to love God, easier to control people than to love people, easier to own life than to love life. Jesus asks, 'Do you love me?' We ask, 'Can we sit at your right hand and your left hand in your Kingdom?' (Matthew 20:21)."

Vote for *My* Jesus!

President Woodrow Wilson is said to have observed that "the silent gospel reaches further than the grandest rhetoric." I have to wonder how this silence would fare in our 24/7, MTV-blaring, white-noise culture. Is there any hope of having a politician give more than lip service to a servant-leadership model fully lived out by the same Lord and Savior that so many politicians quote ad nauseam? What if, just once, those ensconced within the Beltway tried to conduct, say, a Senate subcommittee hearing, a Pentagon briefing, or a Rose Garden bill-signing ceremony with the kind of humility Jesus exhibited?

OK, now I'm really hallucinating. Let's get back to reality here. We still face our original quandary in that we still have to vote. Despite some behavior to the contrary, none of us is God. We all have flaws, and we'll never have a perfect candidate. But let's try to find someone who at least tries to walk the walk.

Alas, I have yet to see a presidential candidate that comes close to fitting this bill, though in 2004 many religious groups produced voting guides designed to help voters take their faith into the voting booth. The Christian Coalition started this phenomenon by pointing out exactly where the godly versus the ungodly stood when it came to issues like balancing the budget, term limits, military spending, abortion, and family values. Anyone who received high marks was deemed "family-friendly" and thus eligible for "official" endorsement (IRS regulations be damned), and those with low marks were labeled liberals—the implication being that they must be defeated at all costs.

Those Bible believers who were really, really godly in the eyes of the Christian Coalition could become church liaisons, who play a vital role in restoring America's God-given glory. After all, according to the coalition, since God ordained government, He therefore ordained our involvement in the governing process. Thanks in large part to the diligent grassroots efforts of the Christian Coalition, Focus on the Family, the Traditional Values Coalition, and other righteous Republicans, the party that abolished slavery has now become so focused on personal morality and the agenda of the Religious Right that it melds the sinners with their sins and opposes anyone who doesn't go along with their conservative philosophies.

Despite what the Christian Coalition may want voters to believe, there isn't an American Republican Standard Version of the Bible. During the 2004 election, organizations like National Council of Churches of Christ USA and Mobilization 2004 published pamphlets that promoted a more progressive scriptural approach to voting according to one's conscience. Also, for Catholics excommunicated from the Catholic League, the Catholic Voting Project offered a comparison chart noting where the U.S. Catholic bishops, George Bush, and John Kerry stood on a host of political issues.

This plethora of voting guides from a wide range of liberally minded sources begs the question, What if the more progressive branch of the church really started focusing on concrete ways to implement the principles outlined in this material instead of devising ways to defeat the Religious Right? Maybe then the church's good deeds and professed tolerance could shine through, and we'd see a truly radical ministry shaped by the love of Christ that could actually, say, eradicate childhood poverty. Remember, it was the church that led the charge to end slavery in the nineteenth century and establish civil rights for all God's children in the twentieth century. Even NRA guru Charlton Heston, then a Democrat and civil rights activist, joined Martin Luther King Jr. in the 1963 March on Washington. He armed himself against the donkeys literally when the Democrats later lost the moral ground it had gained in the '60s by becoming, in the words of California Governor Arnold Schwarzenegger, "girlie men."

So who would Jesus for vote for these days? Being a good citizen, if Jesus came back to earth, He would probably participate in Election Day, though as Alan Storkey observes throughout his book *Jesus and Politics*, Jesus would keep reminding the disciples that His kingdom is not of this world. Like many of us, He might wish there were other candidates on the slate, though I doubt He would voice His disgust with the electoral process by taking His Father's name in vain.

While Jesus kept many of His inner feelings secret, He'd probably give us some political parables to reveal whom He chose as the U.S. leader. And even though deciphering the parables can be a real mystery, based on the cast of characters presented to date as presidential candidates, my hunch is that Jesus would probably be sympathetic to Jimmy Carter's concerns that "there is obviously a widespread, carefully planned, and unapologetic crusade under way from both sides to merge fundamentalist Christians with the right wing of the Republican party. Although considered to be desirable by some Americans, this melding of church and state is of deep concern to those who have always relished their separation as one of our moral values." Let's see. Jimmy won the Nobel Peace Prize in 2002 and like Christ, the dude is one heck of a carpenter.

The Progressive Petition Form Letter

[DATE]

[NAME]

[ADDRESS]

Dear [SALUTATION]:

For the sake of peace, democracy, social justice, and racial equality for all mammals, we oppose the Religious Right's endorsement of [INSERT SPECIFIC POLICY, BILL, DECREE, PLATFORM, COMMENT, OR OTHER ACTION]. Our reasons for protesting this injustice are as follows [CHECK AS MANY AS APPLY]:

___ This clearly violates the separation of church and state.

___ We find no basis for these actions anywhere in the book *Zen and the Art of Motorcycle Maintenance*.

___ This is yet another sign that these fundamentalist patriarchal homophobes refuse to fund our womyn gynocentric vegan lifestyle.

___ It's *my* body, and I'll do what I want with it.

___ Hell no, we won't go.

___ Save the whales.

___ Liar, liar, pants on fire.

___ This is, like, so nonorganic.

___ Bush is the Antichrist.

___ War is not healthy for children and other living things.

___ My brain hurts.

We affirm our unity to each other as communal members living together in perfect harmony. And as such, we will continue our vigilant advocacy efforts to rid ourselves of these unjust zealots. Once these imposters are forcibly removed from office, we will be able to work in solidarity as we fight for a nation built on our self-defined principles of tolerance and love.

United in our fellowship,

Committed to the Cause

Clueless for Christ

So, my guess is that Jesus would cast a write-in vote for former President Jimmy Carter. However, He might ask Carter to stop being such a wuss and do that table-turning-over thing every great once in a while. Let's not relive the wimpy '70s.

Choosing Christ?

Even though Christians talk about following the will of Christ, if He were on the ballot today, would we vote for Him? Hmmm . . . lemme see. Well, for starters, His message is geared toward those "undesirables" who probably aren't even registered to vote. Also, that business of separating the sheep who are eligible to vote for Christ from the hordes of unregistered goats represents a pollster's nightmare.

Let's face it, the dude just can't spin worth diddly-squat. He tells is like it is and doesn't give a rip whom He offends. How can you have a presidential candidate who can't even be trusted to go to a fundraising breakfast and behave in front of the those all-important special-interest groups needed to finance the cost of mounting a presidential campaign? And as much as LaHaye & Co. like to invoke the name of Jesus, there's no way He'd snag an invite to one of those supersecret Council for National Policy meetings (I wish I could tell you what goes on in there, but these meetings are strictly off limits to the media; only individuals with the biggest bankrolls and the best beliefs are allowed access to these contemporary temple treasures).

I don't pretend to know how Jesus would vote. But he surely wouldn't support some of the policies put forth in his name by religious and Republican conservatives. They are contrary to everything he said and stands for.

—Bill Press, "How Would Jesus Vote?"

Now let's examine His staff—oh, just fuggetaboutit. His campaign manager looks like one of those crazy homeless guys I see preaching at Times Square, and His female "companion" has a checkered past that would make Monica Lewinsky blush. He hangs out with tax collectors, drunkards, and a host of unsavory characters. Roger Clinton seems downright dignified by comparison. And last but not least, His "trusted" disciples, the guys He appointed to key leadership positions, make snafus almost every time they accompany their leader in public. (I can just picture all the Christian conspiracy books blasting the behavior of Jesus' cabinet.) Get this—He can't even get any respect in His hometown (sound familiar, Al Gore?).

No, if Jesus stepped into the RNC or DNC headquarters, both Karl Rove and Democratic head honcho Howard Dean would show Him the door fer sure. No way in hell would they even remotely consider His candidacy as leader of the Free World—but then again, Jesus made it clear that His kingdom lay elsewhere.

5

BLESS 'N' BAG BAMBI

The Earth is the Lord's, and all that is in it.

—*Psalm 24:1*

I know that the human being and fish can coexist peacefully.

—*George W. Bush*

What does the Bible say about our obligation to care for all of creation? For that answer, we have to go back to the beginning—the book of Genesis. Now, I don't want to get into a creationism-versus-evolution debate in which we all start fighting like a bunch of unevolved monkeys. Rather, my focus here is on what Scripture has to say about our responsibility to care for the earth once God brought forth vegetation, animals, and all that jazz.

According to Genesis 1:28, God blessed Adam and Eve and said to them, "Be fruitful and multiply, and fill the earth and subdue it; and have dominion over the fish of the sea and over the birds of the air and over every living thing that moves upon the earth." Genesis 2:15 reminds us that even though humans were technically put in charge of the planet, we are not the Lord over all creation. That's God's job.

Rather, we're simply the earth's stewards, summoned by God to watch over and care for all that God created. This implies that God is the landlord, and we are simply the tenants. And even though God said he wouldn't cause another flood, the message that stays with me whenever I read Genesis 6–8 is that God *could* kick us off this planet if we mess up the world to the point where we should be evicted. (The story of Noah also teaches me that if I walk around buck nekkid and drunk, someone "might" choose to report such a misdeed. But that's a topic for another book.)

Seeing that God has entrusted us to be the caretakers of the planet, we need to devise sustainable policies so that our use of the earth's resources will conserve and renew the planet rather than reduce our earthly home to a burnt-out ball of blackened goo. Unfortunately, even though God put us in charge of taking care of his creation, it's pretty clear that we haven't exactly done a stellar job of it.

Throughout the years, we've managed to pollute and distort much of God's creation. The Evangelical Environmental Network's "Declaration on the Care of Creation" sums up our negative effect on creation into the following categories: (1) land degradation, (2) deforestation, (3) species extinction, (4) water degradation, (5) global toxification, (6) alteration of the atmosphere, and (7) human and cultural degradation. What a mess.

To quote Bartholomew, archbishop of Constantinople, "To commit a crime against the natural world is a sin. For humans to cause species to become extinct and to destroy the biological diversity of God's creation . . . for humans to degrade the integrity of the Earth by causing changes in its climate, by stripping the Earth of its natural forests, or destroying its wetlands . . . for humans to injure other humans with disease . . . for humans to contaminate the Earth's waters, its land, its air, and its life, with poisonous substances . . . these are sins." As he points out, our desecration of the very land God entrusted into our care has led us to become in fact "un-creators." Simply put, our need for the earth's resources has reached a saturation point, and we are putting the future viability of the earth in jeopardy.

> Only after the last tree has been cut down; only after the last river has been poisoned; only after the last fish has been caught, only then will you find that money cannot be eaten.
> —Cree prophecy

The Evangelical Environmental Network defines "creation care" as "caring for all of God's creation by stopping and preventing activities that are harmful" (such as air and water pollution and species extinction) "and participating in activities that further Christ's reconciliation of all of creation to God." The group's Web site lists four reasons why Christians should care for God's creation:

1. Christ died to reconcile all of creation to God (Colossians 1:20).
2. All of creation belongs to Jesus (Colossians 1:16; Psalm 24:1).
3. It fulfills the Great Commandments to love God and love what God loves. (It's hard to say you love a child who has asthma when you're the one filling her lungs with pollution.)
4. Pollution hurts the poor the most, and Christians are called to care for the poor and the less powerful (Matthew 25:37–40).

Let's see what Catholics and Protestants have to say when it comes to caring for the earth.

> U.S. Catholic Bishops: "We support policies that protect the land, water, and the air we share. The United States should lead the developed nations in contributing to the sustainable development of poorer nations and greater justice in sharing the burden of environmental neglect and recovery."
>
> National Council of Churches of Christ USA (NCCCUSA): "We are obliged to relate to Earth as God's creation in ways that sustain life on the planet, provide for the [basic] needs of all humankind, and increase justice." This lengthy letter in which this statement appears, signed by major mainline church leaders involved in the environmental movement, included guiding norms for church and society that address the standards and practices of moral excellence that we ought to cultivate in our personal lives, our communities of faith, our social organizations, our businesses, and our political institutions.
>
> National Association of Evangelicals (NAE): "We labor to protect God's creation. Human beings have responsibility for creation in a variety of ways. We urge Christians to shape their personal lives in creation-friendly ways, practice

effective recycling, conserving resources, and experiencing the joy of contact with nature. We urge government to encourage fuel efficiency, reduce pollution, encourage sustainable use of natural resources, and provide for the proper care of wildlife and their natural habitats."

It's pretty clear to me that the vast majority of Christian denominations in the United States support the idea that the Christian community needs to assume its God-given responsibility to start taking better care of the earth.

If anyone can show me where the Bush administration's environmental policy lines up with the any of these organizations' position statements, please do. Given Bush's reliance on the evangelical vote, you'd think his environmental policies would square with the NAE's position statement. But do they? Methinks the answer is, uh, no. That breeze you feel coming from Sagamore Hill in Oyster Bay, New York, is probably committed environmentalist, fellow Republican, and former president Teddy Roosevelt rolling over in his grave.

End-Times Environmentalism

One argument I've heard bandied about by some liberals is that Bush & Co. don't care about establishing environmentally sound policies because "the earth is going to be burned anyway, so why care for it?" In a public speech, Bill Moyers accused James Watt, secretary of the Interior during the Reagan administration, of telling Congress, "After the last tree is felled, Christ will come back." As expected, Watts disputed ever making any such claim, adding that Moyers has since issued a personal apology to him. The online environmental magazine *Grist*, which was the original source of this inaccuracy, has since issued a retraction.

Jim Ball, executive director of the Evangelical Environmental Network (EEN), commented on this he-said, he-said debate, "The issue is not whether some conservative Christians hold what others perceive to be strange end-time views. The issue is whether these views significantly affect their care for God's creation." Even if one does believe that Armageddon is coming any minute, until Christ returns to reconcile all things, we are called to be faithful stewards of God's good garden, as EEN's faith statement puts it.

Even Tim LaHaye, coauthor of the *Left Behind* apocalyptic book series, has said that Christians should work for clean air and water. But just in case there are any members of the Rapture-ready crowd who believe they can shirk their responsibility to look after our planet, please show me *one* verse in the Bible in which God says it's OK to destroy our earthly home in an effort to hasten the coming of Armageddon.

As we all know, Bush plans to open up portions of U.S. wetlands and other previously protected federal lands for commercial use. Yes, I know the information from environmental groups explaining why this is a bad move is filled with technical data, and for those of us without scientific minds, these elaborate spreadsheets can make our heads hurt. But as a layperson, I don't see why we would need to open up lands that have already been determined to need protection.

> We will look upon the earth and her sister planets as being with us, not for us. One does not rape a sister.
> —Mary Daly, *Beyond God the Father*

Now I don't want to come across as one of those crunchy granola lefties—you know, those Earth Mothers in Birkenstocks and patchwork dresses trying to pass off New Age guru-speak as proven scientific fact. But even though I'm a seminary graduate and not a scientist, it just doesn't make any practical sense to me why we continue to engage in antiquated mining practices in search of more fossil fuels such as oil, coal, and natural gas instead of engaging in forward-thinking energy policies. For example, my Google search on the Internet on November 22, 2005, for "hybrid car" produced about 12.9 million hits. Apparently, I am not the only one searching for legitimate solutions to our current energy crisis.

However, I have a sinking suspicion that Bush's environmental initiatives are shaped more by the wishes of the head honchos and major stockholders from Exxon Mobil, Shell, Chevron, and other energy giants that bankroll the RNC than by his personal convictions. Call it a strong hunch. Yes, I know Democrats take money from some really skuzzy and questionable types. And until we get real campaign reform laws passed, this cycle is going to continue. But so far, the oil interests put significantly more money into Republican campaign coffers than they give to the Democrats. As reported by the *Washington Post* on March 27, 2005, "Exxon Mobil, which was the largest contributor among energy companies in 2004, has given $5.2 million to Republicans in the past decade and less than $650,000 to Democrats. Bush received $2.5 million from oil and gas companies for his reelection bid alone."

The bottom line is that many of the federal lands we've taken for granted could become simply a gleam in our eyes, a fond memory that can never be recaptured.

This Time It's Personal

When I was ten, my family bought 125 acres on the side of a West Virginia mountain. Within a year of that purchase, we were forced to sell the land when all the neighbors sold out to a mining company. Next thing you know, the land was stripped bare, and only the Lord knows if that land was ever restored. Not only did I lose out on a newly found childhood fishing and camping paradise, but also I shudder to think of the animals that died not because they were hunted for food but because they were in the path of a giant conglomerate seeking to maximize its profits. Alas, the aftermath of this mining effort not only resulted in irrevocable damage to the area razed, but the air and water were affected for miles in every direction.

I lost my childhood vacation spot thanks to strip mining, and I am tired of seeing too many outdoor recreational areas face ruin in the name of "progress." Unfortunately, I'm by no means the only one who has had a beloved childhood vacation spot despoiled by corporate greed. I wonder for how many more generations we can continue along this path of destruction before there will be no more land left.

Bear in mind that when we're discussing the Bush crew's land management strategies, we're not talking small patches of land here and there. Their approach appears to be more along the lines of a scorched-earth policy than a program that will sustain these lands for use by future generations. To give just one example, in January 2004, Interior Secretary Gale A. Norton cleared a plan to open most of an 8.8 million-acre swath of Alaska's North Slope to oil and gas development. She did this despite the fact that in 1960, President Dwight Eisenhower, another fellow Republican, established the Arctic National Wildlife range "for the purpose of preserving unique wildlife, wilderness, and recreational values." This plan will produce enough oil for six months and will threaten the health of arctic tundra, ponds, and lakes that are home to wildlife and migratory birds for decades, perhaps centuries. Is a six-month supply of fuel worth destroying such a large expanse of God's creation?

Kyoto No-Go

Along those lines, even though Bush keeps telling us he's a "uniter, not a divider," he still refuses to sign the Kyoto Protocol, despite the fact that 153 other countries, including Russia and the entire European Union, have thrown their support behind this document. For those of you who have been relying on U.S. news sources, I don't expect you've heard much in-depth discussion about this amendment to the United Nations Framework Convention on Climate Change. In a nutshell, this amendment to this international treaty on global warming intends to cut global emissions of greenhouse gases.

Jim Ball is right on the money when he makes the case as to why the United States should add its name to this document: "As the world's number-one source of greenhouse gases, America needs to do much more." Here's a stat that blows my mind—the United States, with less than 5 percent of the global population, uses about a quarter of the world's fossil-fuel resources. We burn up nearly 25 percent of the coal, 26 percent of the oil, and 27 percent of natural gas.

But neither Ball's group nor the NAE, two groups that you'd expect our evangelical president to listen to, appears to have influenced Bush's environmental policies. Instead of stepping up to the plate, President Bush appears to be sending the NAE to the showers by choosing to play ball with congressional leaders such as Senator James Inhofe, a Republican from Oklahoma. Inhofe, chairman of the Environment and Public Works Committee, stated in an interview on *The 700 Club*, "We want to have a spiritual country, and I would hate to think that we give in, and particularly to organizations like the NAE, to a bunch of far-left-wing environmentalists." As reported on MSNBC.com, the position paper "For the Health of the Nation" has, he said, "put the NAE at odds with allies of conservative evangelicals in Congress and the Bush administration."

But the NAE membership sure as heck isn't "liberal" by any means. Remember the list of people who signed this document? As I mentioned in Chapter One, the signers include conservative stalwarts like James Dobson, Richard Land, Charles Colson, and Rick Warren. Far left-wingers? I think not.

Even the Christian Sportsmen's Fellowship (CSF) supports the need to take care of the environment—and this from a group of manly men who would probably give anyone a smack upside the head who dared call them liberals. As stated under the mandate of the CSF, "In view of environmental concerns, we as Christian sportsmen accept our obligation to preserve our natural resources and to protect and perpetuate every living species, especially those which are endangered. It remains our biblical conviction that proper ethical behavior when pursuing game, fish, or [fowl] will ensure that future generations will continue to enjoy the hunting and fishing privileges and opportunities that we possess today." (See Genesis 1:27–30 and Genesis 9:1–3.)

Despite that, I don't understand why there needs to be a Sportsmen's Prayer Breakfast during the annual National Rifle Association convention. Are prayers required in order to justify the right of anyone to own a semiautomatic rifle when hunters cannot use these guns legally? And I don't get the need to have *The Camouflage Outdoorsman Bible* nestled in your deer stand, though I'm sure the CSF can explain to me how Bible believers can combine praying and preying.

As I've pointed out, Bush is not the only committed Christian who doesn't give much credence to the creation care movement. Ball has his own opinion on why some conservatives tend to turn their backs to environmental issues: "The main reason many evangelicals have not been as engaged in caring for God's creation as the Bible calls them to be is because in their minds 'environmentalists' are liberals who hold beliefs (e.g. pantheism) and values (e.g. population control) that can be harmful and lead people astray. Indeed, becoming an environmentalist could lead one to become a full-blown liberal, and thus turn away from conservative Christian values and those who hold them." He adds that some evangelicals tend to sound the alarm when they see the liberals employ big government solutions and oppressive regulations as means to solve the environmental problem.

Some of these concerns make sense to me. Even though I'm an avid fly fisher, I've taken to calling myself a "conservationist" as I find myself at odds with the more extreme environmental groups that want to ban all recreational fishing and hunting. And whenever someone starts offering earth-friendly, milk-and-honey-styled prayers in honor of the goddess Sophia, odds are I'll start looking for the nearest exit. But even though we may differ on how to care for God's creation, I pray that we as a Christian community will continue to dialogue in the hope that we can find some common ground here.

Despite conservatives' wariness about being associated with a traditionally liberal cause, Ball believes there's cause for optimism. He writes:

As increasing numbers of rank-and-file evangelical Christians understand more deeply that reducing pollution is loving your neighbor, as they become more aware of mercury's impact on the unborn, that 1 in 6 newborns have potentially harmful levels of mercury in their blood, as evangelicals become more aware that global warming is real and is projected to harm and even kill millions of the world's poorest, whom Jesus Christ identified with himself (see Matthew 25:40), they will become more engaged.

Are there real differences between evangelicals and environmentalists? Sure. There always are between subcultures. Will these differences make us uncomfortable with each other at times? Of course. Is common ground to be found through reducing pollution that hurts people and caring for all of God's creation? Absolutely. The time has come for olive branches all around.

Ever since Don Argue, then president of the NAE, addressed delegates at the National Council of Churches of Christ's annual meeting back in 1996, these two organizations have been extending some olive branches. While great divides still exist between these two groups over issues like abortion and homosexual rights, the environment appears to be an issue on which these two Christian bodies have found some common ground. (By the way, the National Religious Broadcasters, which represents some fourteen hundred broadcast outlets, has since split from the NAE; NRB spokesman Karl Stoll said at the time that some members "felt the NAE was getting too close to the NCCCUSA.")

Unfortunately, it appears that the Bush administration has run out of olive branches and is using a switch instead. Guess the Bushies have finally decided to drop Mother Earth from their cotillion dance card. But instead of sitting like wallflowers waiting for the Bush boys to ask us to dance, maybe we should get up and publicly give some attaboys to the major Christian groups that are dancing to an environmentally friendly tune.

Getting Green for God

For starters, kudos should go to organizations like the Interfaith Power and Light Movement, the Seattle-based Earth Ministry, and other grassroots environmental groups that have diligently advocated for a religious response to the problem of greenhouse gases. Even Bush's buddy Ted Haggard has gotten behind this issue. Apparently, he became passionate about global warming because of his experience scuba diving and observing the effects of rising ocean temperatures and pollution on coral reefs.

A well-publicized and welcome initiative was WWJD (What Would Jesus Drive?), a campaign initiated by the Evangelical Environmental Network and *Creation Care* magazine. The genesis for this project stems from the fact that pollution from vehicles has a major impact on human health and the rest of God's creation. As this initiative notes, "Making transportation choices that threaten millions of human beings violates Jesus' commandments to 'Love your neighbor as yourself' (Mark 12:30–31) and 'do to others as you would have them do to you' (Luke 6:31)." This group contends that vehicles such as SUVs contribute to global warming.

As a nonscientist, I am not equipped to offer a thorough environmental analysis of the role SUVs play in global warming. Even though Catholic priest and sociologist Andrew Greeley and others claim that the link between such vehicles and global warming is fraudulent, most scientists and the majority of environmental groups would beg to differ. The World Health Organization, for one, estimates that up to 160,000 people die each year due to the direct and indirect impacts of global warming, a fact that should give all of us pause.

At any rate, SUVs clearly pollute the heck out of the environment. So why are so many of the behemoths on the road? In addition to emitting noxious fumes into the atmosphere, they are major gas guzzlers. We have a finite supply of gas on the planet, and once it's gone, it's gone for good. However, once gas hit $3.00 a gallon after Hurricane Katrina, sales of SUVs and Hummers started to plummet. Perhaps Americans' changing attitudes toward gas guzzlers may prove to be more than a fleeting change. One can hope.

How much of the earth's resources are we willing to sacrifice just so that we can conform to Madison Avenue's idea of what defines a true-blue American? As evidenced by our consumer culture, even those of us with good intentions often opt for temporal, short-term satisfaction offered by well-advertised products that are image-enhancing but environmentally unsound.

If the mounds of evidence pointing to a dramatic increase in global warming prove to be accurate, we can avert a global calamity by reexamining our transportation options and making wiser choices. If, however, this evidence proves in the end to be faulty, well, we've still cleaned up the environment, and we can all breathe easier. Sounds like a win-win situation to me. (I might add that if I see one more "Hug Your Planet"–style bumper sticker on the back of a gas-guzzling SUV, I may be sorely tempted to run the driver off the road. On second thought, never mind. Breaking one of the commandments just to make an environmental point would make me about as nutty as those Earth Liberation Front fanatics.)

> One day, Christians will look back on the injustices done to animals with the same horror and shame we presently reserve for such relatively recent atrocities as slavery and the Inquisition.
>
> –JesusVeg.com, a Web site sponsored by People for the Ethical Treatment of Animals (PETA)

By "we," I don't just mean society in general but also the church in particular. It's not as if the church doesn't have access to resources that raise awareness of environmental issues. The National Council of Churches of Christ's Eco-Justice Office alone provides a range of environmental initiatives relating to issues such as air and water quality, energy alternatives, public land use, environmental responsibility, Earth Day resources, mercury pollution, and forest protection, as well as a list of denominational resources relating to environmental justice. But despite the availability of all these resources, seldom, if ever, do I see this material placed in the literature racks of local churches. Preserving our planet home, it seems, receives a lower priority rating than, say, the church's latest pledge drive to buy a new organ.

You'll note that I haven't endorsed any particular environmental legislation being sponsored by a given political party. That's because right now, I feel that we as Christians need to first get our own houses in order both in our personal lives and in our church communities. While many churches want to do the right thing and celebrate Earth Day with uplifting and eco-friendly liturgies, I have to wonder about what we're doing the other 364 days of the year.

Examples of churches talking the talk but failing to do the walking thingee abound, but I'll cite just a few. Although a major Episcopal cathedral hired a canon to promote environmental justice, the cathedral itself does not have a long-term recycling program in place. In fact, when I leave most churches, my service bulletin almost always ends up in the trash; there never seems to be a recycling bin nearby. And seldom have I been in a church that offered coffee in something other than a Styrofoam cup or provided a convenient recycling container for soda cans and glass bottles.

One of my big environmental beefs is getting church mailings, press releases, and the like in the mail when the same information could be sent by e-mail, considerably reducing the amount of paper I receive weekly. If an organization—especially a Christian group— must send out mailings, using recycled or recyclable paper makes a whole lot more sense than using nonbiodegradable glossy paper. (As an aside, when I get mailings about the environment from a Christian organization, it would be nice if this material had, oh, I don't know, maybe a *biblical* focus. All too often, I can't tell if a mailing is from a secular environmental group or a religious one. Call me crazy, but I don't think that's too much to ask of faith-based groups.)

For those churches that want to be more eco-friendly, organizations like Green Faith offer practical suggestions for making a

Vegetarianism offers people everywhere important ways Christians may positively impact our world for Christ, by caring for people, animals, and the environment. We believe, therefore, that encouraging plant-based diets is an effective, evangelistic witness to the gospel. It is a contemporary response to Christ's command to "go and make disciples of all nations" (Matthew 28:19).
  –Christian Vegetarian Association

religious community's desire to be more environmentally sensitive a reality. Fletcher Harper, the group's executive director, says people often find that their spiritual life is enhanced when they engage in environmental issues. He adds that that the group's Sustainable Sanctuaries program, which assists houses of worship in modeling environmental responsibility, has the added benefit of attracting people who are committed to the environment and looking for a place of worship that shares this commitment.

[The Japanese word *mottainai*] captures in one term the "three Rs" that environmentalists have been campaigning on for a number of years: *reduce, reuse,* and *recycle.* I am seeking to make *mottainai* a global campaign, adding one more "R" suggested by Klaus Töpfer, the head of the UN Environment Program: *repair* resources when necessary.

–Wangari Maathai, 2004
Nobel Peace Prize recipient

In writing this chapter, I confess I've wasted close to a ream of paper. I tend to write in coffeeshops and public parks where there are no recycling bins available. I haven't walked the walk in other ways, either, so this is an area where I need to get my own house in order. Still, I've tried to offer some resources that have helped me get the ball rolling, and I'm hopeful that the larger Christian community will make use of them as well. More important, I pray that the discussion will continue about the myriad ways we as a Christian community can make an impact when it comes to taking care of our planet. For starters, how about if each one of us makes a commitment to do *something* of a practical nature toward cleaning up our planet? It is our home, after all. Just think what a difference we could make if every church in the country implemented just a few changes. Wow—what an impact!

6

TOO QUEER FOR WORDS

There are about as many sexual identities or sexual
ways of imaging ourselves as there are people alive,
if the truth be known.

—*Carter Heyward, theology professor,*
Episcopal Divinity School, Cambridge, Mass.

When I was at Yale Divinity School, I was coerced into attending a
sensitivity training session during the university's annual Pride
Week. At this rainbow-themed training, I was asked point-blank a
series of questions, such as "Were you born straight, or did you just
choose to like guys?" and "Why can't you just stop dating guys and
go out with women?" and "Why don't you pray that God will heal
you of your heterosexuality?" As a straight female, I confess that I
don't know what it's like to be discriminated against because of my
sexual orientation. But I do know if a cross-carrying stranger came
up and asked me offensive questions like those, all that turn-the-
other-cheek stuff might go out the window and I'd smack 'em one.
I was mightily tempted to do just that to my interrogators at Yale.

According to 2003 FBI statistics, 16.6 percent of the 7,489 bias-
motivated incidents that year were due to sexual orientation. Of the
fourteen bias-motivated murders reported by law enforcement, six
were committed as a result of a sexual-orientation bias. Though
these numbers may be small, I think that we as a Christian community can agree that we should publicly denounce hate crimes of
this sort—especially if they're committed by someone who claims
to be following the teachings of Christ. (And please don't give me

any of that "I killed him because he blew me a kiss" garbage—guys have made all sorts of revolting come-on moves on me, and I've never felt it necessary to pump 'em full of lead).

Frankly, who cares if Adam sleeps with Eve or with Steve? (Assuming, of course, that Adam is not a Roman Catholic priest and Steve is of the age of consent.) As it turns out, a lot of people do care. Once again, the same Religious Right Republicans who decry governmental interference when it comes to religious freedom have no problem whatsoever with governmental interference in the bedroom. Legislating private morality seems perfectly normal to them. Meanwhile, the more extreme progressives expend considerable time, effort, and energy advocating their right to privacy and equality with regard to their morality and sexual orientation, often at the expense of other issues such as the environment and child poverty. Best-selling author Joan Chittister, a Benedictine nun and international lecturer, sums this debate up perfectly: "[This] agenda is simply too narrow, too concentrated on issues around human sexuality alone, and too self-centered to be the agenda that drove Jesus from Galilee to Jerusalem curing lepers, feeding the hungry and raising the dead to life."

> What we are witnessing here are hate crimes against Christianity—the manifestations, the symptoms of a sickness of the soul, a disease a Vatican diplomat correctly calls "Christianophobia," the fear and loathing of all things Christian, coupled with a fanatic will to expunge from the public life of the West all reminders that ours was once a Christian civilization and America once a Christian country.
>
> —Pat Buchanan, "Christianophobia"

But for those of you who require tangible proof, let's look at the facts:

- Number of hits to the Web site http://www.godhatesfags.com: way, way too many

- Number of Episcopalians in the United States: 2.3 million (and declining)

- Number of times retired Episcopal Bishop John Shelby Spong and his progressive pals have pushed the gay agenda to the exclusion of other social issues: roughly, oh, 1.15 million
- Number of times the American Anglican Council and its conservative companions have pushed the gay agenda to the exclusion of other social issues: roughly, oh, another 1.15 million
- Number of closeted Republican members of the U.S. Congress: don't ask, don't tell
- Number of closeted priests and bishops in the Episcopal Church, USA: don't ask, don't tell
- Number of openly gay bishops in the Episcopal Church, USA: 1
- Number of words spoken by Jesus about homosexuality: 0

Now, some Bible believers sport bumper stickers on their cars that say "Jesus said it. I believe it. That settles it." These are the same faithful followers who tend to have their cars adorned with fish logos, WWJD stickers, and other cheesy Christian crapola. I'd like to remind these fundamentalists that when it comes to the issue of homosexuality and the teachings of Christ, "Jesus didn't say it. I believe it. That settles it." Now, can I get an "amen"?

7

JEWS 'N' GENTILES

TIM RUSSERT: Why was it a responsibility, a duty of Christians,
to vote for George Bush?
JERRY FALWELL: Because I'm a Democrat. I don't vote
Republican. I vote Christian. And I believe that he [George
Bush] is pro-life, pro-family, pro-Israel, strong national
defense, faith-based initiatives for the poor, et cetera.
                          —Meet the Press, November 28, 2004

In July 2003, the Israeli newspaper Ha'aretz reported that President
Bush told the Palestinian prime minister, "God told me to strike at
al-Qaeda and I struck them, and then he instructed me to strike
at Saddam, which I did, and now I am determined to solve the
problem in the Middle East." Muckraking master Bob Woodward
comments on Bush's religiously inspired battle plan in his tome
Bush at War: "The president was casting his vision and that of the
country in the grand vision of God's master plan." And based on
Dubya & Co.'s actions to date, it appears as though Bush's interpretation of said master plan features a vengeful Old Testament
God decked out in red, white, and blue and singing The Star Span-
gled Banner as he smites the anti-American infidels.

Maybe my memory has failed me, but I don't recall seeing a
Burning Bush in the Rose Garden or a Mel Gibson–esque Hollywood epic starring George the Younger or any other sign that W
has been anointed a prophet of God. Since when did the Almighty
vest the Bush clan with authority from on high to enact their will—
on an international scale, no less—whenever their advisers feel

moved by the Spirit? And while George W. Bush claims that JC is his favorite philosopher, he seems to have missed those parts that focus on Jesus' love for all of humanity, including His enemies.

As I am not a rabbinic scholar, an expert on the Middle East, or a political pundit, I'd better leave it to the real authorities to provide in-depth analyses of the ungodly mess that's existed in the Holy Land ever since Moses parted the Red Sea and kicked some Egyptian butt. But I think it's important to note what the National Council of Churches of Christ USA (NCCCUSA) and the U.S. Conference of Catholic Bishops have to say on this issue.

First, the Catholic bishops in 2003 urged the United States to "actively pursue comprehensive negotiations leading to a just and peaceful resolution of this conflict that respects the legitimate claims and aspirations of both Israelis and Palestinians, ensuring security for Israel, a viable state for Palestinians, and peace in the region." And the NCCCUSA, an ecumenical organization representing one hundred thousand congregations across the spectrum of orthodox and mainline Protestant denominations, commended Secretary of State Condoleezza Rice's persistent role in facilitating the negotiations that resulted in an agreement related to Gaza's border crossings and movement between Gaza and the West Bank. In a letter sent to Secretary Rice dated November 14, 2005, twenty-one church leaders stated, "We offer our support and assistance, as well as our prayers, as you work toward resolution of this conflict and the building of bridges between the Israeli and Palestinian peoples and the Jewish, Christian and Muslim faiths."

Why is America in favor of Israel? Because we have a great history of biblical belief—Judeo-Christian—and we believe God gave the land to the descendents of Israel. It was not given to Palestine, it *wasn't* given to so-called Palestinians. It wasn't given to Saudis or the Syrians.

   —Pat Robertson

It looks as if the Catholics and the mainline Protestants are in agreement here. If they could just resolve that sticky wine-versus-grape-juice controversy, we'd have it made.

But the true-blue Bible believers have broken ranks with their more "liberal" brethren by throwing their wholehearted support to Israel while thumbing their noses (and worse) at the Palestinians. In 2002, Rabbi Yechiel Eckstein, chairman of the International Fellowship of Christians and Jews, and Ralph Reed, former head of the Christian Coalition, joined forces to create Stand for Israel as a means of mobilizing grassroots Christian support for the Jewish state. This unholy alliance between two religious factions that at their core reject each other's belief system demonstrates once again that religion, like politics, produces strange bedfellows. Lest anyone think this is a small, fanatical fringe group, in 2003 over seven million Christians took part in special services to offer their prayers in observance of the group's International Day of Prayer and Solidarity with Israel.

Such moves, I gather, are a precursor to the end times. But the real sign that the Rapture is coming occurred when Ed Koch, a diehard liberal stalwart and former mayor of New York City, stood at the podium in Madison Square Garden during the 2004 Republican National Convention and endorsed Bush for president. At that moment, I thought for certain I heard the four horsemen of the Apocalypse riding down Broadway. Surely the battle of Armageddon was gonna start at any minute. While I have no hard data on what made Koch, ubiquitous actor Ron Silver, and other prominent New York City Jews join forces with the Religious Right, my guess is they were banking on the fact that in W's quest to see the Revelation prophecies fulfilled, Karl Rove will make sure that Israel becomes 100 percent Jewish, no matter what the cost.

I am not what you'd call a part of the Rapture-ready crowd, but I do try to respect those who, after prayerful consideration, take the book of Revelation literally. (I say "try" because there are only so many times in one day that I can be told I'm going to burn in the fires of hell before I lose both my tongue and my respect for said literalists.) But at the very least, maybe we can agree that for the White House to base its foreign policy on the fictional *Left Behind* series makes about as much sense as conducting an in-depth Bible study using Jenkins and LaHaye's four-novel series *The Jesus Chronicles*. Just a thought.

The government of the Reich, which regards Christianity as the unshakable foundation of the morals and moral code of the nations, attaches the greatest value to friendly relations with the Holy See and is endeavoring to develop them.

–Adolf Hitler, speech to the Reichstag, March 23, 1933

And while we're on the subject of Israel, I wonder if it's possible for Christians to go there without shouting about their faith from the rooftops. Nothing says ugly American, or rather ugly Bible-thumping fundamentalist Christian U.S. citizen, more clearly than, say, passing out Jews for Jesus pamphlets on Yom Kippur, praising Jesus at the Wailing Wall, or singing "Onward Christian Soldiers" as tour groups follow in Jesus' actual footsteps.

Speaking of obnoxious behavior, can you think of anything more offensive and more overdone than the current tendency toward using the terms "Nazi" and "Hitler" in a nongenocidal context? While I will champion everyone's right to free speech, when Democratic leaders such as Senator Robert Byrd of West Virginia and Illinois Senator Dick Durbin compare the Bush administration to Hitler's Nazi regime and Republican Senator Rick Santorum from Pennsylvania calls Democrats Nazis, I'm left scratching my head. While Senate filibusters, judicial appointments, and even the abuses of Iraqi prisoners at Guantánamo should give us pause, in my opinion, they simply do not rise to the level of Holocaust-like atrocities.

I confess that I may have played a small part in this name-calling game. Back in 1995, when the National Endowment of the Arts versus Senator Jesse Helms controversy was at its peak, I penned a piece for *The Wittenburg Door* titled "Ideologically Separated at Birth?" In this article, I compared comments made by art aficionados such as Helms, Pat Buchanan, and Don Wildmon to very similar statements uttered by the likes of Adolf Hitler, Mao Tse-tung, and Senator Joseph McCarthy. My purpose was to point out, in a somewhat satirical fashion, that if we start to muzzle the First Amendment, we could be on this slippery slope that leads to totalitarianism.

And yes, I really enjoy a well done though very un-PC Hitler parody. I laughed myself silly over Mel Brooks's song "Springtime for Hitler" in *The Producers* and giggled when Hitler joined Satan in *South Park*'s rendition of "Christmas Time in Hell." Sometimes der Führer is funny. (Though I gotta admit the two fake Bush-Hitler ads that some wannabe satirists posted on MoveOn.org's Web site were too sophomoric for my taste. If you're going to trash Dubya, try to do something more original than turn the *s* in *Bush* into a swastika. Be creative! But I digress.)

But ever since the 2000 election, there's been an acrimonious bipartisan tone to the point where the Hitler references have gone from satirical to scholarly. When I Googled "Hitler and Bush" on November 23, 2005, I got back over six and a half million hits. Wow. And based on some of these references, it seems like some people are actually taking the Bush-Hitler comparisons as gospel truth.

> If the positive element of Christianity is the love of one's neighbor, that is, caring for the sick, clothing the poor, feeding the hungry, and quenching the thirst of the parched, then we are true Christians!
> —Adolf Hitler, speech to the Old Guard, February 24, 1939

Yes, I've gotten the e-mails, I've seen the blogs, and I agree there are some legitimate concerns that both Bush administrations acted less than honorably. But then again, except for Jimmy Carter, there hasn't been one honest president in my lifetime. Remember, I came of age post-Watergate, so I expect my elected officials to be caught with their pants down and their hands in the till. Just color my generation slightly jaded. The problem for me comes when our religious leaders start acting like politicians to the point where you can't tell who's a preacher and who's a politico.

Living in New York City, I've seen firsthand how the FBI and CIA have pulled moves since 9/11 that give me considerable pause. Still, I don't see where these two organizations parallel Hitler's Gestapo. I've made no secret of my distrust of presidential puppet master Karl Rove. But I would not equate him with Joseph Goebbels, Hitler's right-hand man. True, both men by all accounts engaged in *argumentum ad nauseam*, the name given to the practice of repeating a lie until it is taken to be the truth. However, I've always though of Rove as more akin to, say, the Wizard of Oz than a raving anti-Semite.

That does not mean that we should not be concerned about the actions of the Bush administration and its ties to the Religious Right. Frankly, I wish the mainstream media would pay as much attention to this administration's private affairs as they did to covering Clinton's actual privates. If a Democrat were in the Oval Office, I'd expect just as much scrutiny into his (or her) administration's public policies.

As a journalist, I am appalled that the media are by and large kept in the dark regarding the secret meetings of the Council for National Policy (CNP). As reported by ABC News, "In a 2000 filing with the Internal Revenue Service, the CNP says it holds 'educational conferences and seminars for national leaders in the field of business, government, religion and academia.' Founded in 1981 by Tim "Left Behind" LaHaye, the CNP appears to serve as a place where U.S. conservative politicians, financiers, and religious leaders meet to discuss policy and funding for Religious Right projects. Given that presidential candidate George W. Bush addressed the council members in 2000 and other power hitters have addressed its exclusive membership, there's no logical reason for holding such clandestine meetings.

Even though setting public policy in secret makes my skin crawl, Hitler's creepy slogan "Ein Volk, ein Reich, ein Führer" (one people, one empire, one leader) hardly applies to the Bush administration. I mean, Bush & Co. may make our minds spin, but the fact remains that we can still state our dislike and distrust of the current administration's politics without literally losing our heads. The Bush–Middle Eastern oil ties warrant some good old-fashioned exposés by investigative journalists instead of this *Access Hollywood* fluff we're spoon-fed these days. But in the end, it was al-Qaeda operatives—not the U.S. government—who started this ball rolling on September 11, 2001, and later killed *Wall Street* journalist Daniel Pearl.

So as odious as we may find any U.S. political leader to be, I say we restrict calling someone Hitler unless he's a monster like Slobodan Milošević or Saddam Hussein, who actually ordered massive and horrific acts of ethnic cleansing. And I don't mean to get too radical here, but I think we should put a lid on calling people Nazis unless they are official members of the Nazi Party. There are plenty of other names we can call them if need be.

While we're at talking genocide, I have a question about something that's been bugging me since what seems like forever: why can't our elected officials give more than lip service to the armed conflicts, genocide, and human rights violations that take place in countries that aren't referenced in the Bible and don't produce oil? I mean, think about it: if it looks as if the United States won't benefit financially—or religiously—from a particular conflict, our elected leaders turn around and give the UN a big fat raspberry, as people in less than useful nations continue to die en masse.

We need to realize that given our failure to agree on just what the separation of church and state means, U.S. churches simply have to assume an independent role as advocates for the poor, the victimized, and the powerless in the Middle East and other areas torn apart by conflict and war. And we need to determine what constitutes constructive interfaith dialogue—and then implement it. Let's start by bringing together Jews, Muslims, and Christians in a prayerful attempt to find our common ground as children of God and build on that foundation. I would certainly prefer this kind of honest exchange to gatherings of myopic, like-minded political souls, and I know I'm not alone here. Through my work with *The Wittenburg Door,* I have encountered small pockets of Christians out there who are tired of quasi-religious groups that exist only to advance their own sociopolitical and religious agendas. I don't have the answers, and I doubt that any other individual does either. But as a group, perhaps we can pray and dialogue together in an effort to bring us closer to finding solutions to the complex problems that have plagued too many nations for too long. History is filled with examples of collective Christian contemplation in action, such as the abolition of slavery, the civil rights movement, and the anti-apartheid movement in South Africa. We have the mind of Christ, and we need to act like Christ before time runs out.

An interview with comedian Lewis Black

Excerpted from *The Wittenburg Door,* July-August 1999. Even though this interview was published a few years ago, the themes unfortunately remain relevant.

DOOR: How do you define anti-Semitism?

BLACK: There's a great line I heard from a professor that goes like this: "Anti-Semitism is hating Jews more than is really necessary."

DOOR: Now Pat Robertson has made it pretty clear he wants to Christianize America. It sounds like he wants to take the Jews and send them elsewhere.

BLACK: I wouldn't mind as long as it's a warm climate like Antigua. But I just think that whole thing is so stupid. Pat Robertson is apparently a religious man. So you would expect him to have read the Bible and realize what the deal is. So you'd think he would try to manipulate us in other ways. That's where they lose the power base. Don't tell us to become what you are.

DOOR: Even though Pat thinks the Jews are going to hell, he was one of the religious leaders who embraced Benjamin Netanyahu.

BLACK: Oh, man. It's perfect. When a fundamentalist finally embraces a Jew, he chooses an idiot. I guess they feel like the Holy Land is a mall that has to be protected and that Netanyahu is the best policeman they have for the mall.

DOOR: As you know, there were Americans who were applauding in the street when Rabin was assassinated. Does that make you embarrassed to be a Jew?

BLACK: Yeah! That's amazing. I've had trouble with Israel from the beginning. As I've said, "If you have a desert and you want peace, then you must have gambling." That's what Las Vegas is. I think if they brought gambling to the Holy Land, they'd all be able to live together because they'd be sitting at a blackjack table for twenty-four hours a day.

8

DO PUBLIC SCHOOLS
HAVE A PRAYER?

> You know when prayer was taken out of the schools
> in 1962, it was not really about prayer being taken
> out of the schools; it was a violent assault against
> the future of the kingdom of God—because Satan
> knew if he could take spirituality away from
> children that the next generation would not be
> able to do the kingdom of darkness any damage.
> —*TV evangelist Joyce Meyer, speech at the*
> *Christian Coalition's Road to Victory gathering,*
> *Washington, D.C., October 11, 2002*

I try not to remember my school days. For me, that was a time when cliques ruled and wannabe future writers like me, who saw life just a little bit differently, tended to be ostracized, to put it mildly. No amount of PC policing or Religious Right rumbling is going to change the fact that very often childhood (and adolescence) just plain sucks.

When it came to praying in school, I muttered "God, get me the heck out of here" on more than one occasion. And Lord only knows how many students uttered His name before taking the SATs or other critical exams. And yes, I recited the Pledge of Allegiance every day in school, and despite the claims of too many politically correct educators, saying "one nation under God" didn't turn me into a raving fundamentalist.

A lot of folks on both sides are up in arms about this whole prayer business. Granted, I grew up in the Episcopal faith, where touting one's religion was as gauche as talking about money. So I was never big on public prayers, wearing Jesus junk, or trying to save every soul I saw.

But let's get real here. There are Muslims, Christians, Orthodox Jews, and children raised in other religious traditions in which performing certain rituals or wearing specific items represents an important part of their life. In today's multicultural world, how can our public schools accommodate students who have specific needs based on their religion without imposing those beliefs on everyone else? Now, I would never advocate allowing a child to, say, sacrifice a chicken, smoke peyote, or carry out other religious acts deemed illegal by civil law. No one has ever been able to adequately explain to me what's wrong with giving students a quiet space where they can go to pray either alone or in a small gathering of like-minded souls—especially since schools routinely allocate space to just about every other special-interest group.

On paper, at least, the National Education Association supports the Supreme Court interpretation that the First Amendment "requires public school officials to be neutral in their treatment of religion, showing neither favoritism toward nor hostility against religious expression such as prayer. . . . The First Amendment forbids religious activity that is sponsored by the government but protects religious activity that is initiated by private individuals, and the line between government-sponsored and privately initiated religious expression is vital to a proper understanding of the First Amendment's scope." So as long as the school doesn't sponsor or endorse a religious event and we all play in our respective sandboxes without throwing sand at each other, we should be A-OK. Seems reasonable.

The problem appears to be with this First Amendment thingee— what constitutes free speech when said speech could hurt someone's feelings or be deemed offensive. As a religious satirist, it's pretty clear I tend to stand on the side of arguing that if you don't like the music, either change the channel or tune it out. Thanks to my diverse educational experiences, I've had a long history of arguing with PC professors and Bible-thumping proselytizers. This background gave me the backbone that enables me to write for *The Wittenburg Door*. But even more important, having some rather wacko ideas thrown repeatedly in my face taught me to think about why I believe what I do. I learned the art of discernment and the need to examine both sides of a given issue instead of simply mouthing whatever mumbo-jumbo I heard coming from any given teacher or preacher.

Keeping the Faith?

Some folks believe that wearing "Jesus Saves" T-shirts or other outward expressions of Christian faith can be seen as offensive to people who don't buy into the God game. When it comes to the whole Christian marketing thing, much of what is sold as holy should be given to the dogs (paraphrase of Matthew 15:26). But these items strike me as no more insipid and silly than, say, donning an "Anarchists Unite" black armband or showing off your intellectual superiority by sporting a shirt emblazoned with a photo of your favorite dead Communist.

I, for one, tend to get more offended by the sight of someone's boxer shorts or thong coming out of his or her pants or T-shirts that tell me what Bush can do to himself. Also, maybe I'm missing the boat here, but I don't see how you can ban Christian gear unless you're going to impose a strict, uniform dress code that includes banning items like yarmulkes, turbans, and other religiously symbolic articles of clothing.

For those Christians who want to share their faith in school, Jesus does issue some pretty clear directives here. While we can't expect teens to act like full-fledged adults, it seems as though that some Christian role models for these kids kinda ignore the Savior's advice. In Matthew 6:5–6, He lays it on the line: "And whenever you pray, do not be like the hypocrites; for they love to stand and pray in the synagogues and at the street corners, so that they may be seen by others. Truly I tell you, they have received their reward. But whenever you pray, go into your room and shut the door and pray to your Father who is in secret; and your Father who sees in secret will reward you." How about if we agree that students can

MICHAEL MOORE: If you were to talk directly to the kids at Columbine or the people in that community, what would you say to them if they were here right now?

MARILYN MANSON: I wouldn't say a single word to them; I would listen to what they have to say—and that's what no one did.

–From the Michael Moore documentary *Bowling for Columbine*

pray but no one should be forced to listen to them? As George Carlin aptly proclaims, "Thou shall keep thy religion to thyself!!!"

I admit that what I'm asking for here is nigh on impossible. After all, no matter how much you try to get kids to "behave," let's face it, teens—Christian and otherwise—tend to be, well, overenthusiastic and at times even downright obnoxious. If they're not sporting a WWJD bracelet and shoving "The Four Spiritual Laws" in your face, they're blasting Marilyn Manson and wearing ripped "Your Savior Sucks" T-shirts. And if the valedictorian's speech at graduation isn't overflowing with the joy of Jesus, they're reciting Green Day's "American Idiot." They're rebelling. That's what teens do.

Can we save the confiscating and banning biz for when they bring to school, say, guns, drugs, and other implements that really might hurt someone? I have had so many people say countless obnoxious things to me over the years. While years of hammering at my psyche did turn me into a religious satirist, I'm still a believer, albeit one who follows her own spiritual path at times. And to my fellow brothers and sisters in Christ, isn't our faith strong enough that we can all see through this silliness?

Thou Shalt Not Teach Religion?

And another thing I've noticed is this move by some school districts to sweep religious history under the rug. What's going on here? I mean, a quick romp through history clearly demonstrates the role that religion has played in conflicts and conquests. I'm related to three pilgrims; Roger Williams, who founded of the state of Rhode

Island; and, rumor has it, the abolitionist leader William Lloyd Garrison; and it wasn't until I began investigating my family tree that I learned the extensive role religion played in the founding of our nation and the abolition of slavery, among other pivotal events.

Apparently I am not alone in my assessment here. William Nord, a religion professor at the University of North Carolina at Chapel Hill, is among the scholars struck by the fact that the powerful and politically correct multicultural movement "has virtually ignored religion, but religion often is more important in defining people's identifies and values than are race, class, and gender." So the question I would pose to educators is, "How can we place religion in its historical context alongside the myriad other factors that influenced major movements both in the United States and throughout the world?"

The religious battles have reached full-scale guerrilla warfare when it comes to teaching that man evolved from monkeys. Now, when I went to school, the creation-versus-evolution debate never really materialized, though the behavior of some of the high school athletes' pretty much disproved Darwin's survival of the fittest theory. Again, I'm no scientist, but it seems to me that there is a limit to what scientific disciplines can objectively prove. When it comes to a questions like "OK, so what started the universe?" I remember my science teachers telling us over and over again that while there are many theories, there is no universal consensus within the scientific community as to what started this whole ball rolling.

At least for me, exposure to the flat-earth folks, creationists, and the intelligent design community have expanded my intellectual horizons. However, suggesting that perhaps we teach scientific theories in, say, science class and then teach nonscientific but widely held views such as intelligent design in a history or social studies class tends to get both the PC police and the conservative Christian crowd up in arms.

Also, the conservatives tend to sound the red alert around any mention of sex education, homosexuality, or condoms in schools. (Amazing, isn't it, how sex continues to be the one hot-button issue that gets the conservative engine all revved up? By the way—if you want a really good laugh, try sitting through a lesson on the birds and the bees taught by nuns like I had to do.) Conversely, I've seen my fair share of pandering to the PC crowd by promoting a curriculum designed to help kids improve their self-esteem and awareness about how their bodies work but which in reality rendered them unable to function once they graduated into the "real world."

As I've noted, my public school education (with a bit of Catholic schooling thrown in as a guilty pleasure, I guess) exposed me to a wide range of people with different belief systems, cultural backgrounds, and the like. While this exposure at times drove me nuts, I was at least somewhat prepared to face a diverse world upon graduation. If you prefer that your child refrain from interacting with anyone who doesn't meet your rigid moral standards, then I guess there's always home schooling or private school. Having said that, I'm not sure that protecting your child from any and all of life's temptations is going to help that child deal with the real world.

But given the amount of white noise around this debate, perhaps we need some real prayer here. Let's all say together the prayer Jesus taught us . . . (Matthew 6:9–13): "Our Father . . . (This prayer was interrupted suddenly due to a potential lawsuit from the American Civil Liberties Union, I guess because the words *Jesus* and *prayer* give the ACLU the heebie-jeebies. Also, the Young Life crowd cited me for using the New Revised Standard Version of the Bible when every true believer knows that saved teens find more salvation when they use Thomas Nelson's *Revolve* Bible. Excuse me, I mean "Biblezine.")

Random Thoughts on Evolution

In the beginning, when God created the heavens and the earth, the earth was a formless void, and darkness covered the face of the deep, while a wind from God swept over the face of the waters. Then God said, "Let there be light," and there was light.

–Genesis 1:1-3

If people want to believe what may well be the case, that God created every-thing, that's OK by me. But when they begin to say that we should not teach what 98 percent of American scientists do believe, then we have a problem.
   —Steve Allen

Man is descended from a hairy, tailed quadruped, probably arboreal in its habits.
   —Charles Darwin, *The Descent of Man*

This monkey mythology of Darwin is the cause of permissiveness, promis-cuity, prophylactics, perversions, pregnancies, abortions, pornography, pol-lution, poisoning, and proliferation of crimes of all types.
   —Judge Braswell Dean, Georgia Court of Appeals

My theory of evolution is that Darwin was adopted.
   —Comedian Steven Wright

It's the lie of evolution that all men are just evolved and that they're all equal and that all creatures are equal.
   —Tim LaHaye, coauthor of the *Left Behind* series

A biologically static world would leave a Creator's creatures with neither freedom nor the independence required to exercise that freedom. In bio-logical terms, evolution is the only way a Creator could have made us the creatures we are—free beings in a world of authentic and meaningful moral and spiritual choices.
   —Kenneth R. Miller, *Finding Darwin's God*

Both sides ought to be properly taught . . . so people can understand what the debate is about.
   —George W. Bush, when asked if children attending public schools
      should be taught intelligent design alongside evolution

We promote the scientific evidence of intelligent design because proper consideration of that evidence is necessary to achieve not only scientific objectivity but also constitutional neutrality.
   —Intelligent Design Network, Inc.

(continued)

I was taught that the human brain was the crowning glory of evolution so far, but I think it's a very poor scheme for survival.
   –Kurt Vonnegut Jr.

I'd like to say to the good citizens of Dover: if there is a disaster in your area, don't turn to God; you just rejected Him from your city.
   –Pat Robertson, responding to Dover, Pennsylvania's voting its
     school board out of office because its members supported teaching
     intelligent design

9

GET A LIFE

Let's face it, moral discourse in most of our churches is but a
pale reflection of what you find in *Time* magazine.
—*Stanley Hauerwas, United Methodist pacifist and theologian*

In our thirty-second-sound-bite-saturated culture, we expect instant
answers to even the most complex of life's problem. However, questions like "Why are we here?" "When does life begin?" and "Is
Snoopy in heaven too?" represent the type of deep theological topics that have occupied the minds of philosophers and theologians
ever since God kicked Adam and Eve out of the Garden of Eden
and told them to get a life.

Frankly when it comes to this whole pro-life/pro-choice fracas,
I'd love to do one of those *Bewitched* moves—you know, just wiggle
my nose and make the whole subject vanish. As an avid fly fisher,
I'd much rather have a debate about whether or not I should row
versus wade a given body of water instead of parsing the nuances of
a discussion about the landmark 1973 Supreme Court decision that
has divided the religious community like nobody's business. In fact,
one of my concerns is that whatever I say here can and will be used
against me by other Christians to prove whether I am innocent or
guilty of following their version of Christ's teachings.

But OK, here goes. First off, if we as Christians believe that God
is the Creator of life, then that means life is a gift from this loving
and gracious God. I am humbled by the thought that, wow, I'm here
on this planet as a living and breathing person made in the image of
God. Think about how mind-blowing that is. And when I say life,
I am referring to the time between the moment we became a twin-
kle in our mother's eye until the second we draw our last breath.

Although I am no scientist, it appears that once the sperm and egg stop doing the mating dance and get down to bidness, what ends up being produced is a baby. (Interesting how creationists support science when it affirms their beliefs that life begins at conception but then they debunk the largely accepted scientific theories of evolution. Go figure.)

Anyhow, as scientists note, this "substance" is a fertilized egg. This means it's an itty-bitty kiddy and not a blob of tissue, a failed medical experiment, or a fetus in a Mason jar to be used for demonstration purposes. Some pro-choicers eschew the term *abortion*, preferring more pleasant-sounding phrases like "termination of pregnancy" or "the right to choose." These terms make an abortion sound almost appealing—you know, like one of those ocean breeze–filled feminine hygiene ads. That kind of talk merely serves to mask the harsh reality that this is a bloody medical procedure with some real health risks, a tragic choice that no woman would willingly make unless she felt she had no other, more palatable option.

Furthermore, the "it's my body; forget about the baby" argument troubles me. As much as I'd like to champion my right to do as I please, this me-ism seems contradictory to the teaching that Christians are one body in Christ. I take this to mean that as followers of the teachings of Jesus, we have a collective responsibility to care for one another. Unless we consider an unborn baby to be a nonperson, I would include that baby as part of this Christian body. Having said that, watching a predominantly male pro-life leadership dictate how women should conduct their lives really gets me steamed sometimes. Compassionate conservatism? I think not. Let us not forget that this pregnant woman is also a member of the body of Christ. Simply put, she needs our love, compassion, and care as she makes an excruciatingly painful decision that will remain with her for the rest of her life.

Choices? What Choices?

The reasons women choose to have abortions are as individual as the women themselves and include financial concerns, family pressure, problems with the baby's father, and fear that they will be unable to

care properly for the child. Carlton W. Veazey, past president of
the Religious Coalition for Reproductive Choice, says, "We must
acknowledge that poverty, physical and sexual violence, lack of
education, poor health, lack of
affordable child care, and other
economic and social injustices
affect women's options and decisions about child bearing." People
who want to make abortion safe,
legal, and rare pay too little atten-

Let us go forth to the city, the
barrio, the urban center, the sub-
urb, and the village, to let every
American woman know that her
decisions, including her choice
for abortion, are her right and
responsibility as a being created
to think, discern, and choose.*
    —Religious Service, March for
        Women's Lives, Religious
        Coalition for Reproductive
        Choice, April 28, 2004

tion to the *rare* element. So the challenge I would pose to all parties involved in this debate is to reduce the number of unwanted
pregnancies by diminishing the obstacles that make women feel
they need to seek out an abortion in the first place.

According to many in the pro-family crowd and select Monty
Python fans, every sperm is indeed sacred, but the social policies
they endorse seem to say "fuggetaboutit" once the baby is born.
Why are the unborn cherished and crack babies neglected? The
same people who stand outside abortion clinics shrieking "Stop the
baby killing!" are often the very ones championing Republican-led
programs that cut vital health care services that could actually prevent children from dying. Furthermore, these zealots decry programs that offer contraceptives and other preventive measures that
could reduce the number of unwanted pregnancies. I'm not saying
all pro-lifers are like this; pro-life groups like Feminists for Life walk
the walk on a consistent basis by promoting solutions to the abortion dilemma, such as improved child support legislation and affordable day care programs.

In fairness, I don't see the Democrats advocating very strongly
here when it comes to legislation around issues of poverty. If politicians

---

*Am I the only one who is more than a little bit creeped out by this prayer? I'm into free
will and all, but something just ain't right here.

really care about the fact that more than one-third of children in the United States live in low-income families, they sure as heck have an odd way of showing it.

The standard pro-life response to the woman facing an unplanned crisis pregnancy appears to be, "Well, if you can't afford to keep the child, then just put it up for adoption." To me this is a case of cuddly-critter syndrome—everyone wants the puppy with the shiny coat and the wet nose, but no one wants to touch the mangy dog that's limping and has pink eye. There's a great demand for healthy children, but not so much for children born with mental and physical problems. God bless the few who are willing to take these children of God into their homes and raise them. But we all know that these are the babies who are most likely to end up getting shuttled around from foster home to foster home until they end up in jail, on drugs, as unwed parents, or all of the above. And the cycle continues.

Many Christians who believe that the woman has to carry the child to term and then either raise the baby herself or give the infant up for adoption have demonstrated that they are willing to embrace and support this pregnant woman. She will be understandably lonely, confused, and frightened during this nine-month period. If she chooses adoption, she will still face nine months of potential ridicule from friends and coworkers. Family members may view her as a fallen woman who should be punished for her sins. Also, those around her may view her pregnancy as an unnecessary financial drain on their already limited resources. And to top it off, she will face the immense sorrow of giving up her baby. Throughout the years, I have encountered a number of church ministries that help pregnant women cover their medical expenses and other financial costs associated with carrying a child to term, as well as giving them a shoulder to cry on when the going gets rough.

Unfortunately, not all churches pitch in to offer practical help. Let's say the woman decides to keep her baby. Who will come forward and be the extended family to help her care for this child over the next eighteen years? In addition to spiritual and emotional support, she's undoubtedly going to need practical assistance ranging from parenting education to donations of baby clothes to babysitting services, and the list goes on and on and on. Until the church can really be the church by being a loving, supportive, and nonjudgmental community that's willing to walk beside these sisters in Christ, I fear that women facing a crisis pregnancy will continue to resort to what they see as a last, albeit horrific, option and abort their child.

When dealing with a woman facing a crisis pregnancy, simply handing her a pamphlet with the phone number of her friendly neighborhood abortion clinic or trying to coerce her into the arms of a potential adoptive family seems to me to be more patronizing than pastoral. If you watch pro-life and pro-choice protesters raising a ruckus outside an abortion clinic or protesting during a rally, *pastoral, compassionate,* and *Christlike* aren't the terms that come to mind.

While we're at it, I'd like to propose that the entire Christian community give a dishonorable discharge to the Army of God, radical right-leaning vigilantes who promote "eye for an eye" justice in the abortion debate. While the vast majority of pro-lifers condemn abortion bombings and other acts of violence, anyone who claims to be a Christian and yet thinks it's somehow OK to kill a doctor who performs an abortion should be publicly branded a hypocrite and not elevated as a martyr for the cause.

Onward, Christian Soldiers

For citizens on the conservative front, the U.S. Supreme Court went to hell in a handbasket when it legalized abortion in 1973. *Roe v. Wade* marks the moment that women's rights and abortion rights won the day and family values vanished. James Dobson and his family-friendly crowd have a long history of misinterpreting "family" and "values." But then again, what can you expect? These are the dudes who outed SpongeBob SquarePants and Tinky Winky and even boycotted Mickey Mouse, but they let that phallic-looking cucumber featured in the family-friendly Christian cartoon series *Veggie Tales* stay in the cartoon closet.

Clearly, abortion is the fertile field that has united conservative Catholics and the Religious Right. According to the Republican National Committee's Catholic Task Force mission statement, "We have studied the political records of all major parties and we believe that the Republican Party is closest to the teachings of the Catholic Church." Ahem. Wait a minute. You've got conservative evangelicals who are so eager to preserve the life of unborn babies and yet they jump at the opportunity to fry sinners joining forces with the Catholic church, which has taken a strong stance against the death penalty.

Are conservative Catholics so desperate to prohibit abortion at all costs that they are willing to form alliances with those who advance policies that are diametrically opposed to the full range of Catholic social justice teachings? Judging from the looks of it, I'd have to say the answer is yes.

To Live and Die in America

Currently, extremists on both sides of the life debate have made abortion such a pervasive issue that other life-related issues, such as the death penalty, stem cell research, and the right to die, often get lost in the shuffle. In fact, the loud roar of extreme voices has become so deafening and polarizing that the voice of reason has come down with laryngitis trying to compete. Joan Chittister summarizes this apparent dichotomy: "We are so concerned about abortion but seem to not realize that what we have already aborted is the rest of our moral value system. What is happening to a real concern for the full spectrum of life issues, the full scope of biblical morality, once so well defined by Cardinal Joseph Bernardin, if only some parts of life were worthy of protection?"

Whereas we now have the technology to prolong life, the ethical framework for dealing with this technology lags far behind. Lord knows Congress and the White House could benefit from a reasoned and civil dialogue with religious leaders from different faith traditions in dissecting the scientific versus moral implications of the whole stem cell debate. Some conservative diehards like Nancy Reagan, Senator Arlen Specter of Pennsylvania, and Senate Majority Leader Bill Frist appear to think that developing treatments using stem cells that could help millions of Americans who suffer from rehabilitating diseases is indeed a "pro-life" position. Other conservatives disagree, noting that Christians have an obligation to preserve life at all costs. Patrick J. Mahoney, director of the Christian Defense Coalition, flatly stated that Frist cannot be both "pro-life and pro–embryonic stem cell funding." Religious leaders can play a vital role in helping decipher the complex medical maze involved in determining when life truly ends.

When I worked in hospitals as a chaplain and a social work intern, I was surprised at how many people thought that a "do not resuscitate" (DNR) order was a death warrant and that by signing a living will, patients were in fact giving the OK for their relatives to off them. These are difficult medical issues, but pastors can help patients and their families understand them so they can make informed decisions about their future.

The Terry Schiavo international media circus demonstrated just how divided Christians are when it comes to determining the moment when our lives on earth end and hopefully our lives in heaven begin. This tragic case represents yet another dysfunctional family dynamic that had heartbreaking consequences. Many Americans agree that this situation should have been handled privately by the family, in consultation with the medical profession and the clergy. But let's be honest here: it's unlikely that this case would have gotten national attention and requests for governmental intervention if Terry had been a non-Caucasian who resided anywhere but Florida, the state where Baby Bush serves as governor. But given that Dubya owes his presidency to Jeb and the Religious Right, there's no way he could let this one slide. This case proves that conservative evangelicals are all gung ho when it comes to states' rights—except, of course, when they don't approve of what the state is doing.

> Can dedicated Christians step into this process and say we have now reached the point in human development where we have not just the right, but the moral obligation, to share life-and-death decisions with God?
>
> —Retired Episcopal Bishop John Shelby Spong

Even though just about every other right-to-die case is handled in private, Terry's saga became a national debate. This means that Jesse Jackson had to get into the picture (go figure) as he preached about the need to extend the metaphor of Terry's feeding tube to feeding the entire world. "Those on food stamps need a feeding tube to fend off poverty and starvation. Our homeless population needs a feeding tube to extend their lives and survive." I think most if not all of us can safely say that if we find ourselves in a vegetative state, we would prefer to keep the media, Jesse, and other self-interested parties out of our hospital room so we can die in peace.

Finally, since all life is sacred, who, if anyone, should make that dreadful and agonizing Sophie's choice on when to end life? I am not so sure I trust the U.S. government as the final arbiter in making such a gut-wrenching decision. Let's face it: despite any moral message a politician may preach as he panders to his constituency, we can't be blind to the fact that money is a huge factor in this debate. According to the *American Journal of Medicine*, health care lobbyists spent $237 million—more than any other industry—to influence U.S. senators and representatives, the White House, and federal agencies in 2000, an election year. Something tells me what these guys are peddling is legislation that is cost-effective rather than life-affirming. If I am ever faced with these gut-wrenching life-and-death decisions, I pray that I will be surrounded by a group of loving and discerning Christians and a compassionate doctor instead of bureaucrats who have been lobbied to death.

Bridging the Gap

Complex moral issues like these require us to engage in prayerful analysis instead of getting ready to rumble. As we pray about these dilemmas, I suggest that we as Christians change the focus of this discussion so that we are no longer adversaries sharpening our swords for battle. The vitriolic material I've been receiving from both liberal and conservative Christian groups surrounding the Supreme Court nominations to fill the vacancies left by Justices Rehnquist and O'Connor tells me that this abortion battle threatens to erupt into a full-scale war. Let's turn down the shouting and then begin to pray together as brothers and sisters in Christ. If we can be still and let God enter into the conversation, perhaps we can really hear each other and begin to seek out common ground.

Lest Christians feel that the gulf between these two camps cannot be resolved, organizations such as Search for Common Ground offers practical and reasonable solutions for how individuals of different faith traditions and belief systems can find areas of mutual interest even when dealing with an explosive issue like abortion. For example, the Common Ground's *Network for Life and Choice Manual* highlights a case study that demonstrated how pro-life and pro-choice Christians in Buffalo came together in 1999 following the murder of abortion doctor Bernard Slepian. The participants identified seven shared areas that create a basis for cooperation:

1. Promoting both male and female sexual responsibility
2. Fostering equality and respect for women
3. Strengthening parent-child communication
4. Reducing the number of teen pregnancies
5. Improving prenatal and maternal care
6. Supporting and funding the choice of adoption
7. Working together to remove the conditions that lead to abortion

If we truly want to follow the teachings of Christ, let's put down the picket signs and download a copy of this manual (you can find the Internet address in the endnotes). Seems to me we'd be all better off dialoguing instead of demonstrating. Just a thought.

An Interview with Flip Benham

Flip Benham is the director of Operation Save America (formerly Operation Rescue). This interview was first published in *The Wittenburg Door,* September-October 2000.

DOOR: Not everyone agrees when life . . .

BENHAM: You are seeing before your very eyes the Gospel battle and the Gospel lines drawn in the very same way that they were in slavery. And you are seeing incredible amounts of bloodshed with these little baby boys and girls. Now we are seeing kids applying the abortion solution to other problems.

DOOR: If you'll just permit me . . .

BENHAM: They are shooting their friends in school because they are angry at their friends or jealous of a boyfriend. Murder has become the solution for everything. If you want a plain cheese pizza, you just kill the Domino's pizza guy and eat. Basically, life has been cheapened because we have not rightly represented the Gospel of Christ. So when we point the finger in Operation Rescue, we point the finger directly at ourselves. It is the Church of Jesus Christ that has allowed us to enter into this mess. And it is only the Church of Jesus Christ, not the president, not the Supreme Court, and not the Congress, that's gonna get us out of this mess.

DOOR: While you're inhaling, what did the church do that you claim was so wrong?

BENHAM: Simply by being ashamed by God's word and this wicked and adulterous generation that was turning from Him. In the 1960s, I can remember very well being a part of the free-love movement. Do whatever you want. Have sex with whomever you want. We're barnyard animals after all; if it's warm we have to copulate.

DOOR: !!!

BENHAM: And so there needed to be a solution for some of the consequences of that sin. Nature abhors a vacuum, and an enemy came in.

DOOR: And . . .

BENHAM: God has been replaced with metal detectors, drugs, violence, condoms, pregnancy, and abortion because we have just removed

God from having any word in our society. He's not important. He's trivial. We need to satisfy our flesh, and who knows better than us how to satisfy it. The problem is that there are consequences to our sin, like little babies that are born. But our kids are paying for the sin of fathers, who are no longer home. They are busy making money and doing their own thing and siring more kids and then getting abortions for them.

DOOR: Now . . .

BENHAM: This whole moral breakdown has just destroyed the character of this nation until God says, All right. You want to see what you are. I'll put him [at] 1600 Pennsylvania Avenue and you can look at you. And see how much you like what you've become.

DOOR: Clinton . . .

BENHAM: Of course the answer is, the polls say that so long as he's doing a good job, it doesn't matter what he does in his private life. Now God says that what you do in your private times is what you really are. "Blessed are the pure in heart for you shall see God." Well, the fact is that none of us have a pure heart anymore, and the church certainly doesn't because the church hasn't rightly represented God. And so we have allowed this camel to get his snout in the tent and now he's taking over the whole tent.

DOOR: Wait . . .

BENHAM: You allow this solution for our promiscuity to kill the very young and we'll end up killing the very old. And now we've found a solution for Down syndrome babies called amniocentesis. We've overcome Down syndrome by killing Down syndrome babies. What we have become are barbarians in pinstripe suits strutting around with briefcases and little laptop computers. Now that's an incredible thing to say to a people that feel that we are so civilized.

DOOR: Can we . . .

BENHAM: But nobody has killed with such ease as many as we have. Nobody! God tells us in his scripture that the kindest acts of the wicked are cruel. The wicked being those who depart from his principles. So look at our kind "I feel your pain" acts. We want to pass out clean needles to people that are strung out on drugs

(continued)

because, after all, they might get AIDS and it's such a compassionate thing. It is not. It is the ultimate act of cruelty because you will
not love that person enough to confront that person and deal with
the sin that is destroying him and destroys a nation that approves
of that behavior.

DOOR: Back to abortion . . .

BENHAM: Affirmative action is another one of the kindest acts of the
wicked. It seems so good to promote this person because of his
color and not make him meet certain standards because of the
way he looks or his national origin. So therefore we promote
[people like this] and they become dependent upon a government
rather than dependent upon Christ. Welfare is another kindest act
of the wicked. It seems so right that we help our brothers and sisters, but what happens is that welfare creates an incredible depen-
dence upon a government rather than on God. And so instead of
turning the hearts of the people toward God, it turns the heart of
the people toward Uncle Sam.

DOOR: So you're equating abortion, affirmative action, and welfare
with . . .

BENHAM: So instead we're passing out condoms to our kids because
we've thrown up our hands in moral surrender and said in
essence to them, "You're barnyard animals. If it's warm you will
copulate, so here's some of these things and hope you avoid the
consequences. And if you don't protect yourself, we've got another
solution. It's called murder."

DOOR: . . . Sounds like you're trying to embrace a whole array of family
values issues, thus diluting the militant message of Operation
Rescue that was embraced under your predecessor, Terry Randall.

BENHAM: ——

10

BAGGING THE BEATITUDES AND WORSHIPING THE ALMIGHTY DOLLAR

The Beatitudes

Blessed are the poor in spirit, for theirs is the kingdom of heaven.

Blessed are those who mourn, for they will be comforted.

Blessed are the meek, for they will inherit the earth.

Blessed are those who hunger and thirst for righteousness,
    for they will be filled.

Blessed are the merciful, for they will receive mercy.

Blessed are the pure in heart, for they will see God.

Blessed are the peacemakers, for they will be called children
    of God.

Blessed are those who are persecuted for righteousness' sake,
    for theirs is the kingdom of heaven.

Blessed are you when people revile you and persecute you
    and utter all kinds of evil against you falsely on my account.

Rejoice and be glad, for your reward is great in heaven,
    for in the same way they persecuted the prophets who
    were before you.

—Matthew 5:3–12

When I was a kid, I felt blessed whenever I entered "pretty church"—proper pipe organ music, the 1928 *Book of Common Prayer,* Easter lilies, tea with cucumber and watercress sandwiches—you know, the works. On those Sundays when my father would score a gig as a supply priest at one of the chichi churches, I was in southern society heaven. But most of the time, he preferred to work in urban churches devoid of any traditional Episcopal trappings. While I hated going to those "less desirable" churches, I realize now that despite the peeling paint on the walls, threadbare carpets, and dilapidated pews, the Gospel was lived out every single day in these real houses of God.

As I've gotten older, I've learned I'm by no means the only one who preferred "pretty church" over the real deal. When I was at Yale Divinity School, I was surrounded by a number of students who were the "pits" (priests in training). Many of these pits plotted out their future in the ministry as though they were climbing to the top of the corporate jungle. The end goal was to become the rector (CEO) of a wealthy parish or perhaps even bishop or dean of a cathedral. The idea that Christ may have been calling them to a less affluent ministry never seemed to cross their minds.

> God works where there's faith. And faith to me is having a positive outlook, believing that things are going to get better, and expecting good things in life.
>
> —Joel Osteen

At the seminary dinner hall, discussions about the church pension fund and clergy compensation packages all too often took priority over brainstorming innovative plans for creating dynamic ministries. At times, I felt that books like *Jesus CEO: Using Ancient Wisdom for Visionary Leadership* and *God Is My CEO: Following God's Principles in a Bottom-Line World* were cherished more than the Bible.

At that point in my spiritual walk, I was still somewhat intrigued by those wealthy, endowed parishes that appeared to cross party lines. I knew I had the right stuff to fake it as a socially acceptable WASP. In these churches, the limousine liberals sip sherry with their moneyed Republican counterparts. Clearly, the focus for these churches was on maintaining a hefty endowment and creating an edifying country club type of church that soothed the social register without scolding the sophisticated. Just as in the White House and on Capitol Hill, the real God worshiped in these churches was the almighty dollar. However, those who lacked the funds to join the frozen chosen were not invited to the tea party, just as those without the financial means to lobby for their interests continue to be ignored by both political parties.

During one summer, I worked at a wealthy D.C.-area parish, where I was stunned at the perks the clergy were able to score. Clergy should receive adequate compensation and perhaps even benefits such as a discount on their children's tuition at schools and camps affiliated with their denomination. But let's get real. Do they really need to enjoy a lifestyle befitting the CEO of a Fortune 500 company? I don't see why a church should bankroll mansionlike rectories, tens of thousands of dollars in private school tuition, country club memberships, expensive dinners at the best restaurants, and the like. Yes, Virginia, I have witnessed all that and more.

Examples of this kind of abuse abound, but one illustration should suffice. Here in New York City, we have an Episcopal church that owns more than six million square feet of commercial real estate, thanks to a land grant given to the church by Queen Anne in 1705. That makes the church one of New York City's largest corporate landlords. A quick look at its grant distribution program shows that it doesn't come remotely closely to tithing its income. And the perks and housing that this parish's CEO/rector gets are simply mind-boggling. Let's just say that he lives much better than the majority of his parishioners do.

Of course, I had to obtain all of this financial information second-hand. When I was writing some articles focusing on post-9/11 ministries, I asked the church's communications department for a copy of the church's financials and other material that most churches have readily available. My requests were met with a haughty response that would have made any Anglophile proud. I have since learned that I am by no means the only seeker who has been shown the door.

Is Jesus One of Us?

I am trying to imagine Jesus addressing a group like the Consortium of Endowed Episcopal Parishes, but I keep laughing so hard my sides hurt. For starters, I am not even sure He would get an invite.

An Interview with Betty Bowers, America's Best Christian

Excerpted from *The Wittenburg Door,* July-August 2002

DOOR: What's the difference between a Counterfeit Christian™ and a True Christian™?

BOWERS: If I can see you when I turn my head in selfless acknowledgment from my reserved pew (row A) during services, you are a True Christian™—even if you slight Jesus by sitting all the way back in the $75 seats.

DOOR: How do you define CHARITY?

BOWERS: CHARITY is a well-known acronym for Christians Having A Righteously Itemized Tax Year. As True Christians™, we are called upon to help feed the hungry because when the underclass is sated, they are far less likely to steal your Prada handbag.

DOOR: How do you interpret Jesus' command for the rich man to give up all his wealth and follow Him?

BOWERS: As with all instances when Jesus appears to veer recklessly from the Republican Party platform or ask the onerous or inconvenient, we must call up the Holy Spirit to flutter on our shoulder and interpret Scripture nimbly enough to invert its apparent meaning. For example, when Jesus asked all those who followed Him to give away all their possessions, He was speaking to His disciples, who were all notoriously poor. None had a summer home on the Dead Sea. Therefore, in asking them to give away all they had, He was simply asking them to give nothing to the poor, since that is precisely what they had to give. As a Republican, I try to follow this glorious tradition.

DOOR: Explain the origins of your Christian crack whore ministry.

BOWERS: To spend half the evening on your knees without praying struck me as an appalling oversight of a glorious opportunity to multitask.

DOOR: Why are you opposed to the work of Habitat for Humanity?

BOWERS: The Lord Jesus was rather emphatic: "The poor will always be with you." I would never do anything that would risk turning Jesus into a liar, dear.

I doubt Christ would own the right Armani suit and silk tie needed to gain access to a gathering of this nature. But assuming the consortium members let Him in, my guess is Jesus would ask them why they are focusing on the bottom line while their membership numbers continue to evaporate. I mean, what's the point of a pretty church if there is no one in the pews?

I've seen firsthand how easy it is to get sucked into this culture. For several years, I lived with my grandparents in their chichi country club home. Also, for a while I belonged to both the Yale Club and the New York Junior League. The longer I stayed within this subculture's rigid confines, I found myself thinking more about how to be "in" rather than focusing on the needs of people who were standing on the outside looking in.

I am well aware that circulating among the moneyed set can enable a sincere soul to secure significant and much-needed funding that can be used to bankroll noble projects. People who have been blessed financially have performed countless acts of financial generosity throughout history. And I have seen some wealthy parishes become so transformed by the concept of *missio dei* (God's mission) that they genuinely began to put their money and their faith into practice.

Maybe some people can float among the social register crowd and keep their faith intact. But for me, I had to leave that cloistered environment. I could feel myself becoming the snotty, elitist type of Christian that I knew was anathema to the Gospel teachings of Christ.

As much as I tend to poke fun at the frozen chosen Episcopalians, there are plenty of other churches that spend a fortune on glitzy worship services, dazzling TV graphics, and hotshot singers and preachers—and then fork over diddly to outreach efforts. This desire to create pretty churches appears to cut across denominational lines.

Mike Yaconelli preached against equating affluence with God's favor. "I've heard God credited for getting new cars, new houses, new clothes, even new girlfriends. What I would like to know is why God is so good at providing new cars and boats and so bad at feeding most of the world. I think the answer is obvious. God isn't the infinite Santa Claus. God doesn't give people material abundance as a reward for serving him. We have taken our material-obsessed mentality and tried to make the Christian faith compatible with it. That just doesn't work. Material abundance says nothing about God's blessing, and we dare not equate the two."

Buddhist monk and author Thich Nhat Hahn states in one of his fourteen precepts, "We are determined not to use the Buddhist community for personal gain or profit, or transform our community into a political instrument. A spiritual community should, however, take a clear stand against oppression and injustice and should strive to change the situation without engaging in partisan conflicts." The same concerns could be expressed about the Christian church. (BTW—shame on any self-righteous Christian who feels that by quoting a Buddhist monk, I'm now a heathen. Countless Christians have benefited immensely from applying Buddhist principles to their prayer lives. Maybe if instead of making demands on God all the time those judgmental Christians tried centering prayer, a form of prayer that allows one to be still and listen to God, perhaps they wouldn't be so self-centered. Uh-oh, looks like my own judgmentalism is acting up again. I clearly need to center myself right about now.)

So WWJD if He stepped inside one of these pretty churches? We do know in the Gospel of Luke that when it was pointed out that the Temple was adorned with priceless stones and gifts dedicated to God (sound familiar?), Jesus replied, "As for these things that you see, the days will come when not one stone will be left upon another; all will be thrown down" (Luke 21:6). I know that the standard interpretation of Luke 21 is that it refers to the Second Coming, when the things of this world will vanish. But I'll bet if Jesus had really been impressed with the majesty of the Temple, He would have said something to that effect.

Jesus, Alias the Temple Terminator

Instead, as Jesus demonstrated through His earthly ministry, He chose to drive out the moneychangers and anyone else He felt was keeping people from coming to His altar. (See John 2:14–16 for starters.) And as the Gospel indicates, the only time we see Jesus really lose His temper is when the religious elite tries to create a church that soothes and satisfies the socialites while excluding those deemed to be "unacceptable" because of their race, social standing, financial resources, and other human-made barriers.

Based on Jesus' teachings, I'll bet that if He were around today, He'd denounce any church that elevated parishioners to a favored status simply because they made a substantial financial donation. I don't think Jesus would be thrilled one bit at seeing major donors being rewarded with key committee appointments, pew assign-ments, rector teas, and other earthly pleasures, while the less desir-ables sit in the back row wondering if they are "worthy enough" to receive communion.

Even though there are over three thousand references to poverty in the Bible, almost all politicians and too many Christians treat poverty as though it was a dirty little secret, a word that can-not be mentioned in polite society. Many churches do admirable grassroots work on behalf of the poor, but all too often the church misses the boat by ignoring the poor or giving them Bibles in lieu of food. Some churches choose to make donations to help the less for-tunate, but then parishioners get upset when the poor "disrupt" their worship and try to become actual members of their church community.

Jesus lays it on the line in the Beatitudes (see Matthew 5:3–12), which is where we started this chapter. In that passage, Jesus states point-blank who is blessed in the eyes of God and shifts the social paradigm by putting the "Temple rejects" front and center in His ministry. For me, that's the underlying beauty hidden in what I call the stewardship guilt passages—you know, those verses that are strutted out each year when a congregation has its annual Steward-ship ("Give me money *now!*") Sunday.

In the story of the widow's mite (see Mark 12:41–44 and Luke 21:1–4), Jesus notes that while the powerful and politically con-nected patrons dropped off a certain amount of money into the col-lection box, a destitute widow gave to God all she had.

Barney the White House Dog Reviews Jim Wallis's Best-Seller *God's Politics*

As barked to Becky Garrison. Originally posted at TheCheers.org, April 18, 2005.

Every time any wuss says George W. Bush isn't acting like a Christian, I start growling and try to bite 'em. Uncle Karl Rove said I'm such a faithful watchdog that he appointed me to be the spiritual sniffer to the President. As the First Doggie, I get to smell all this sacred stuff that W doesn't wanna look at cause it makes his head hurt.

And I just finished smelling this really big book called *Dog's Politics.* Woof—a book just for me. I started sniffing around *Dog's Politics,* but then I took one bite and spit it out. Blah. It tasted like granola and kinda smelled like this stuff I saw Jen smokin' one day. My mommy, Laura, said *Dog's Politics* would taste better if it was published by InterVarsity—she thinks the people at HarperSanFrancisco are going to H-E-double toothpicks 'cause they put out books by "liberals" that don't love Jesus. And my mommy is a librarian so she knows what she's talking 'bout.

Now, I really tried to eat *Dog's Politics,* but on every page I tried to nibble on, this Wallis dude is saying something mean about my daddy, Dubya. I don't get it. I mean, I get to live in the White House—and this Jimmy guy wants me to go live with these people that look like hippies. No way. They smell funny—kind of like Rev. Jesse Jackson. W says that Jesse stinks!

You know what's real fun to eat? My daddy's *Revolve* Bible. It's got pretty pictures and quizzes and all kind of fun things in it. Mommy Laura said it's from Thomas Nelson, so it's gotta be righteous and really Republican. Kewl. Yummy. I also like to eat the pages outta Grandpa Tim LaHaye's book *The Rising*—oh, boy, those pages taste super sweet. Grandma Beverly said this book'll take me right straight to doggie heaven.

Anyway, one day the President got real mad at Tony Campolo 'cause Tony was telling him how sinful his budget was. I tried to mount Tony, but that mean man kicked me. So Karl, Dick, and Daddy came to my rescue, and they threw copies of *Dog's Politics* at Tony. Then this Campolo crybaby started yelling something about "compassionate conservatism, my ass." Daddy said only Uncle Dick is allowed to swear in the White House. So Uncle Karl told me to let Tony have it. I bit him as hard as I could, but I don't think I like Tony—he tasted real tough and gave me a tummy ache.

No matter what the godless heathens might say, my daddy, Dubya, treats me like I'm a little angel. He tickles my tummy, gives me Rold Gold pretzels, and even lets me come to meetings and do my bidness whenever there's donkey types in the room. Uncle Dick put a copy of this book in my wee-wee corner—he said I should start doing my bidness on *Dog's Politics* instead of going on the *Washington Post* all the time. 'Nuff said.

Thomas Keating offers this comment on the story: "We might take these two small coins to stand for what constitutes human nature, namely, body and soul. She had no superfluities, that is to say, she had nothing to offer except body and soul. But because it was all she had, she put in more than all the others."

For those with earthly eyes, a woman like this, who could only offer to God her poverty, loneliness, and weaknesses, doesn't represent "our kind of people." But Jesus saw through her outward appearance to what lay underneath. He saw her humble heart, which was ready and willing to give all she had to God. Keating notes, "Jesus' doctrine goes right to the heart of reality and presents us with true values, cutting across all sham, show, superficiality, and the accidental. 'My son, give me the gift of your heart.' That is what he wants. With that gift he can add everything else. But without it, our score will always be very low no matter how much the audience may applaud."

Let's move on to the rich man, needle, and camel scenario (see Matthew 19:16–24, Mark 10:17–25, and Luke 18:18–25). This scene starts out innocently enough. A wealthy and seemingly virtuous young man tries to find out from Jesus what he needs to do in order to get to heaven. Jesus tells him to keep the Ten Commandments, follow the Greatest Commandment—and give up his possessions. Although the young man was willing to follow the commandments, he balked at giving up his prized possessions. He walked away unable to accept the greatest prize of all. Jesus could see into this young man's soul, and there He saw how his riches enslaved him. He knew that in order for this man to be truly

Our country puts $1 billion a year up to help feed the hungry. And we're by far the most generous nation in the world when it comes to that, and I'm proud to report that. This isn't a contest of who's the most generous. I'm just telling you as an aside. We're generous. We shouldn't be bragging about it. But we are. We're very generous.

–George W. Bush, discussing faith-based initiatives with urban leaders, July 16, 2003

free, he had to release himself from these attachments. And just as it's pretty darned impossible for a camel to go through the eye of a needle, Jesus knew that this young rich dude couldn't give up his earthly possessions without some divine intervention.

The story of Zacchaeus underscores the teaching that all things are possible with God—and that a rich man actually *can* enter the kingdom! (See Luke 19:1–10.) Zacchaeus, a despised tax collector, experienced a genuine conversion when he gladly accepted Jesus into his life and then agreed to not only give away half of his possessions to the poor but also to repay fourfold every person he had swindled. He had very little left in terms of worldly possessions, but Zacchaeus' joy demonstrated how Christ can transform a person's mind and heart.

In the Sermon on the Mount (see Matthew 5–7), Jesus turned the world upside down and inside out by emphasizing values that are pretty much the opposite of what the world deems to be of importance. According to Jesus, the poor, the humble, and the peacemakers were the blessed ones. Furthermore, Jesus made the point that whenever we provide for the physical needs of the least of these, we in fact come face to face with the living Christ (see Matthew 25:35–40).

Talkin' the Talk

One portion of the National Association of Evangelicals' position paper "For the Health of a Nation" outlines this organization's stance when it comes to addressing the issue of poverty: "By deed and parable, He taught us that anyone in need is our neighbor (see Luke

10:29–37). Because all people are created in the image of God, we owe each other help in time of need." To this end, the NAE "urges Christians who work in the political realm to shape wise laws pertaining to the creation of wealth, wages, education, taxation, immigration, health care, and social welfare that will protect those trapped in poverty and empower the poor to improve their circumstances."

This position statement appears to be somewhat in opposition to an open letter signed by more than eighty evangelical leaders that stresses the importance of relying on biblical values in selecting candidates on Election Day. This letter lists six issues that should shape voters' decisions—the Supreme Court, terrorism, abortion, gay marriage, embryonic stem cell research, and environmental development. Poverty did not make the list. Now, given that some of these signers are also members of the NAE, I am sitting here scratching my head wondering how come they kinda sorta forgot what the NAE says here about the need to take care of "our neighbor."

Prior to the 2004 election, the Alliance to End Hunger and Call to Renewal conducted a survey in which they discovered that a majority of voters—78 percent—said a candidate's plan for fighting poverty would affect their voting decision, while only 15 percent said a candidate's position on gay marriage would matter. But as Jim Wallis says, "I don't hear Bush ever talking about the Sermon on the Mount; I just don't hear it. I'm hard-pressed to think of teachings of Jesus that are being talked about in the White House." Once again, the Bush administration appears to have blown off the NAE.

> A nation that continues year after year to spend more money on military defense than on programs of social uplift is approaching spiritual death.
> —Martin Luther King Jr., "Beyond Vietnam"

Meanwhile, the Democrats appear to be blowin' in the wind. They protect their turf by supporting stagnant and failing social institutions because they feel they can take the liberal and progressive vote for granted. Simply put, they seem to be more concerned with maintaining the status quo than winning the war on poverty.

Ever since Clinton declared himself the family-values candidate in '96, the Democrats have tended to position themselves as "Republican Lite" instead of articulating their own moral vision for America.

"Poverty" Is *Not* a Four-Letter Word

Even though our two-party system has kicked the poor to the curb, the poverty stats keep staring me in the face. The Center for Public Justice's chilling report "Hunger No More," issued in the summer of 2005, states that "worldwide, 10 million children die every year from preventable causes. Over 800 million people suffer from hunger. In 2003, more than 36 million people, including 13 million children, were at risk of hunger in the United States. One in four people in a soup kitchen line is a child."

Ron Sider, president of Evangelicals for Social Action and a thorn in the side of the evangelical movement since he penned his best-selling book *Rich Christians in an Age of Hunger* in 1977, comments on the government's lack of concern to address the issues surrounding poverty: "What I deplore is a failure to have the right kind of public policies that guarantee that any American who works full-time responsibly would get out of poverty and have affordable health insurance. Millions of Americans work full-time and do not even earn enough to reach the poverty level. Forty-five million lack health insurance. For the richest nation in history, that is blatantly immoral." How can anyone claim that the United States is guided by "Christian" principles when, as our laws demonstrate, our political leaders have so clearly bagged the beatitudes in their quest to line their own pockets?

As Wallis crisscrosses the country preaching his antipoverty message, he points out that "budgets reveal our priorities as a family, a church, or a nation. In evangelical language, the proposed [2004] budget from the Bush administration is 'unbiblical.'" In her column "From Where I Stand" dated February 17, 2005, Joan Chittister echoed that sentiment: "National budgets are a nation's theology walking." Well, if that's the case, then it looks as if Uncle

Sam's been spending a bit too much time bellying up to the bar because our country sure as heck is walking crooked.

On December 23, 2002, Bush received a Christmas present of sorts when religious leaders representing a wide spectrum of the faith community sent him a letter asking that the federal budget for fiscal 2004 take into account the needs of low-income working families. In this letter they told the president:

> We share your commitment based on religious conviction to bring about positive change, and the faith community will continue to show compassion to our neighbors in need. But as we continue to serve people in poverty, we also recognize the need for systemic change to reduce poverty. As we act to the fullest extent possible within our means, we urge you to do the same. We also reaffirm our commitment to working with your administration on public policy initiatives that will help alleviate poverty. If given the chance, the faith community can continue to provide valuable ongoing guidance through principles born of a deep religious faith and an understanding of helping others.

For those who feel the church and nonprofit social sector can pick up the slack created by these draconian budget cuts, Wallis cautions against making a blanket assumption that faith-based organizations have the financial resources to cover any gaps caused by federal budget cuts. "The president's faith-based initiative is fast becoming a hollow program that merely provides equal access for religious groups to the crumbs falling from the federal table." As the reduction in the federal budget trickle down to the state level, Wallis adds that these cuts "will be acutely felt by faith-based service providers who will bear the brunt of increased poverty in their communities." Along those lines, while churches and faith-based organizations—not FEMA—responded to the massive immediate needs of those who lost everything in the aftermath of the 2005 hurricanes, no church or nonprofit entity can be expected to address the long-term needs caused by a catastrophe of this magnitude.

By the time the Bush administration released its 2006 proposed budget, many religious leaders felt that the United States was walking backward. In an April 2005 letter sent to President Bush, the heads of the Episcopal Church, the Presbyterian Church (USA), the United Church of Christ, the Evangelical Lutheran Church of America, and the United Methodist Church wrote, "If passed in its current form, [this budget] would take Jesus' teaching on economic justice and stand it on its head." They added that "the 2006 budget had much for the rich man but little for Lazarus" (see Luke 16:19–31).

However, according to the Bush White House, Lazarus is being taken care of here. The president's budget message, February 7, 2005, states that the 2006 budget "affirms the values of our caring society. It promotes programs that are effectively providing assistance to the most vulnerable among us." The Democrats on the Senate Budget Committee responded the next day proclaiming, "If we pull back the curtain on President Bush's FY 2006 Budget, we see that it would further worsen the nation's fiscal outlook."

Although I'm a satirist, not an economist, it seems to me that cutting or eliminating programs that benefit the poor and the middle class while at the same time providing tax cuts for the wealthiest Americans is laughable, even ludicrous. But that doesn't mean that I'm ready to swallow whatever political pabulum the Democrats are trying to spoon-feed me either. I graduated to the adult table a long time ago, thank you.

But I get the strong sense that some of my Christian brothers and sisters on both sides of this Bush budget business would prefer to sit at the kiddie table. Some of the e-mails I've been getting these days from Christians who are either blasting Bush or damning the Democrats make me embarrassed at times to call myself a Christian. I've already admitted that as a religious satirist, I have a heckuva time trying to live out this Greatest Commandment thingee. And it's especially hard for me to extend the hand of Christ's love toward those in the Beltway when I see pictures of people dying as a result of bad public policy. But before we come to blows, it might be a good idea for Christians at both ends of the political spectrum to stop throwing temper tantrums and spend a bit of time praying together in a nonpartisan timeout corner.

Will We Walk the Walk?

A diverse group of evangelical leaders, including Southern Baptist leader Richard Land and Wallis, sent a letter to President Bush on January 17, 2005, in which they urged a strengthened, expanded emphasis on overcoming poverty both here and abroad over the next four years. Even though these two men are often pitted against each other in debates, they were able to come to some agreement regarding the issue of ending poverty.

From June 4 through 7, 2005, Call to Renewal and Bread for the World, the nation's largest grassroots lobbying organizations on domestic and international hunger issues, cohosted "One Table, Many Voices: A Mobilization to Overcome Poverty and Hunger." This first-ever Interfaith Convocation on Hunger at the Washington National Cathedral included more than forty heads of faith communities. Leaders from Jewish, Catholic, Orthodox, Protestant, Muslim, Sikh, and Buddhist traditions prayed and advocated for the end of hunger in the United States and beyond. Antipoverty slogans, campaigns, and initiatives discussed at this conference included Hunger No More, Make Hunger History, Make Poverty History, the One Campaign, and the Micah Challenge.

Maybe I'm being really naive here, but I believe that just as the churches united to bring about the civil rights movement back in the sixties, we can unite to end hunger. Bread for the World states on its Web site, "The United Nations Development Program estimates that the basic health and nutrition needs of the world's poorest people could be met for an additional $13 billion a year. Animal lovers in the United States and Europe spend more than that on pet food each year. What makes

> Where God is, there is love; and where there is love, there is always an openness to serve. The world is hungry for God.
> —Mother Teresa,
> *No Greater Love*

Jesus began to weep.
—John 11:35

the difference between millions of hungry people and a world where all are fed? Only a change in priorities. Only the will to end hunger."

Now that we have the will, I pray that God will show us the way.

тhe republican-democratic joint program to eradicate world hunger and achieve world peace

1.

2.

3.

4.

5.

6.

7.

Note: When the Republican National Committee was asked what the respective political parties are doing about joining forces with the religious community to achieve lasting peace and end famine throughout the world, "reliable RNC authorities" hinted that this program is under prayerful consideration. However, it appears as though this program has been "Scootered" for the time being. The RNC reports that for the immediate future, its slate is full as it is sponsoring ethical seminars for the White House staff, coaching Supreme Court nominees, and training chaplains to minister to the needs of its flock, who are facing indictments and other legal woes at the hands of the demonic Democrats. Inquiries to Democratic National Committee headquarters on June 9, 2005, were met with an answering machine message featuring DNC chair Howard Dean in full rant mode: "We will not play with this white, Christian party! I have a scream!! AAAAAHHHH!!!!!"

11

WHERE IS THE LOVE?

> I hope Americans will continue to pray that
> everyone in my administration finds wisdom and
> always remembers the common good.
> —*George W. Bush, "Words from the President on Prayer"*

President George W. Bush says he views religion as a personal matter: "I think a person ought to be judged on how he or she lives his life or lives her life. . . . Faith-based is an important part of my life, individually. . . . I don't condemn somebody in the political process because they may not agree with me on religion."

James Dobson echoes Bush's sentiment: "Pluralism is part of our system. We don't all think the same thing, and part of our strength is that we come from different perspectives. We have to respect one another even when we disagree with each other. There has to be a spirit of tolerance for the views of others while also being deeply committed to the positions we hold. If we do that, I think we can coexist and learn to love each other better."

Now that I've recovered from spilling my morning coffee all over myself, I can hear Thomas Paine wailing in the background, "Of all of the tyrannies that affect mankind, tyranny in religion is the worst." First off, let me stress that I agree in principle with what Bush and Dobson are saying here. Seriously. I do. And I really, really, really wish that I could believe these two brothers in Christ. But I can't. But let's just say that based on what I've seen of their actions to date, they aren't exactly practicing what they're preaching here. It's that talk-the-talk, do-what-I-say-but-ignore-what-I-do type of deal all over again.

But Bush and Dobson are by no means alone in their desire to be "Christian" but in their daily actions fail to be, well, "Christlike." My guess is that very few of us actually wake up and decide that we're going to blow off the teachings of Christ and follow our own whims instead. Speaking for myself, I know that more often than not, I find myself thinking, "I can't believe I just did that." Like Bush and Dobson, I want to extend Christ's love in a particular situation, and but my ego keeps getting in the way.

> Religious people love to hide behind religion. They love the rules of religion more than they love Jesus. With practice, Condemners let rules become more important than the spiritual life.
> —Mike Yaconelli, *Messy Spirituality*

All too often, I see instances where the church fails to extend Christ's love and radical hospitality to the strangers in our midst. When I walk into most churches these days, the congregation makes me feel like I just crashed some private members-only party. What's worst, though, is when the ushers look at me as if I just stepped in something and they wish I'd get my smelly self out of their sanctified sanctuary.

I admit I've been love-bombed by some conservative churches, especially of the charismatic variety. At first, these faith communities will offer me a warm, fuzzy sense of belonging. But then they start talking about Satan, sin, the role of women, the biblical mandate to spank children, and of course, the rapture. Their leaders make it pretty clear that if I want to continue to receive their blessings and affections, my beliefs had better line up with theirs. These churches seem to confuse being righteous with being right, leaving no room for debate. Yeah, they love me, but only on the condition that I'll buy into their interpretation of Christ's teachings.

A recent, well-publicized example of this dynamic in action took place in North Carolina. (I hate to say this, but as a former North Carolinian, this comes as no surprise.) Chan Chandler, the pastor of the East Waynesville Baptist Church, led the charge to kick out nine church members who refused to support President Bush during the 2004 election. Yale Law School professor Stephen Carter notes that in a case like this, like it or not, the state has no right to tell the church what to say. He goes on to say, "The idea that a government benefit—such as a church's tax-exempt status—might be conditioned on speaking the right words from the pulpit is odious."

But (and this is a really big *but*) even though I support congregations' right to worship as they please and would not want to impinge on their beliefs, I don't think Jesus came down to earth and gave His life just so that people could be excluded from *His* altar. (FYI—for those of you who think that the church belongs to you, sorry. Last time I read the New Testament, it was still Christ's church.) Let's get real here. Seriously, are issues such as judicial filibusters, the Marriage and Family Act, and other nonessential matters really worth dividing us as a Christian community? Carter cautions, "If we take the next step and close our doors because of political affiliation, both democracy and the churches are the losers."

There is a fine line between witnessing for the Gospel and creating a set of partisan criteria for who is welcome at a particular church's table. As much as I've been slamming Bush, Dobson, and the conservative crowd, this problem presents itself in the liberal community as well. Too many seemingly open-minded clergy have a strong territorial need to safeguard their strategic position within the DNC hierarchy. They only trash Republicans, without bringing their own party to task. Also, just about every self-proclaimed liberal clergyperson I have met has this obsession about not offending someone. That's understandable, but then they try to "compromise" by acting "inclusive" and "tolerant" to the "other." (This professed tolerance, however, does not extend to Republicans and southerners, whom they see as fair game for attack.) I know of interfaith dialogue sessions, but more often than not, what I've seen is that these meetings end up being rap sessions among like-minded folk without the presence of their more conservative faith partners.

Easy to Be Hard

Why do we find it so hard to love those with whom we don't see eye to eye on political issues? Authors Daniel Homan and Lonni Collins Pratt offer these insights in their book *Radical Hospitality: Benedict's Way of Love*: "Our closest relationships are built on what we share and have in common. We build relationships at work, school, church, and in our neighborhoods. We meet people while we serve on the board of some local charity or in a service club. Thus we form a social sphere of people who are like us and do not feel like actual strangers."

But as Homan and Pratt point out, "The problem with this manner of forming relationships is that we may exclude those who are not like us. We don't exclude those intentionally, but our worlds tend to be small and homogeneous. We don't go looking to be made uncomfortable." After 9/11, at least here in New York City, there was a sudden rise in the sale of "comfort food." For a brief moment, items like banana pudding and other foods that evoked fond childhood memories flew off the shelves. At the same time, area churches were flooded with spiritual seekers looking for a safe sanctuary, though it appears that church attendance has returned to a pre-9/11 level.

It's a natural human tendency to seek out "comfort" to help us feel secure when we're frightened and feel that the world is closing in around us. Our innate need to be comforted because we're afraid causes us to form a tightly knit prayer circle around those who look, think, and act like us.

However, this action means we exclude those who are not part of our "family." Homan and Pratt reflect, "If we consider the possibility that others do not feel and think the same as we do, we suddenly feel very small in a mysterious, expansive universe. There is a security in a world where all the others are like me. It's a false security, but we prefer it to no security at all." So we band together with like-minded believers in a concerted effort to ward off our perceived enemies. It's us against the world—reason and compassion be damned. These groups tend to be governed more by fear than love, and as time goes by, they all too often become more closed, isolated, and rigid in their acceptance of any outsiders, whom they see as posing a threat to their "community."

Brian McLaren reminds us that if churches become preoccupied with the question of who's right to the exclusion of considering whether they are truly good (as in "bearing good fruit"), they're destined to fade, wither, and fail. "To the degree that they have sold their spiritual birthright for a political ideology, they must repent; neither left nor right leads to the higher kingdom."

So what does God expect of us as a Christian community? Correct me if I'm wrong, but I don't see anything in the Bible addressing the issue of partisan politics. In fact, Jesus makes it pretty clear that we are to render under Caesar that which is Caesar's and render under God that which is God's (see Matthew 22:17–21). And unless I'm missing the boat here totally, I do think one role the church has is to be prophetic—to speak truth to the powerful and hold the government's feet to the fire when our elected leaders neglect any segment of society. I don't see how the church can have a prophetic voice as long as it remains hostage to the particular whims of a political party—which as we all know is controlled in the end by the interests of those who bankroll the whole business of politics.

Instead of engaging with believers from different political backgrounds to find common ground to begin a civil discourse on complex moral issues, too often Christians confuse acceptance of others with approval of their position. They become so obsessed with being right that they refuse to graciously acknowledge those whose political views diverge from their own. How can the Christian community hope to come to any common ground and engage in civil discourse when the very places of worship where Christians gather are not welcoming to brothers and sisters of different political persuasions?

> How then does love conquer? By asking not how the enemy treats love but only how Jesus treated it.
>
> —Dietrich Bonhoeffer,
> *A Testament to Freedom*

Radical Hospitality

What does it mean to extend hospitality to people we dislike? While noting that the enemy is often defined by the political order, Homan and Pratt challenge Christians to search for some degree of real acceptance that allows them to offer a genuine word of welcome to those with whom they disagree. "By accepting someone, we do what seems to be a small ordinary thing. A simple act would seem to be small anyway, but little acts of giving, one upon another, pile up to create a huge force capable of repelling darkness and transforming the world."

What if, instead of creating political havens where political souls gather, churches chose to receive others based on the Greatest Commandment of all, as expressed in Matthew 22: 37–39? Simply put, as Christians, we are commanded to "love God with all our heart and all our soul and love our neighbor as we love ourselves." 'Nuff said.

As Henri Nouwen said, "Hospitality means primarily the creation of a free space where the stranger can enter and become a friend instead of an enemy. Hospitality is not to change people but to offer them space where change can take place." If we can embrace our political rivals by creating such a sacred space, then perhaps we will find out for ourselves that the radical hospitality of Saint Benedict offers a much needed power for both the church and the world.

Right about now, my cynical self is telling my idealistic self to go take a hike. In the song styling of Tom Lehrer, "Oh, the Protestants hate the Catholics. And the Catholics hate the Protestants" . . . you get the drift. Believe you me, I know it's hard as all get-out to love people that you don't like one bit. When I interviewed Madeleine L'Engle, I asked her how she could forgive someone who had wronged her. She answered me point blank: "I remember someone who had done something very awful to one of my children. And I was very angry at him. So I said, 'God, forgive the bastard.' And that was enough. It was a start." Christ never said we had to like that you-know-what. And I don't see anywhere in the New Testament where Jesus uses phrases like "Have a nice day," "Don't worry, be happy," and "Smile!" Rather, He says that we are to extend His radical love to all of humankind. And by default, that would include those from opposing political parties.

OK, I know some of you are going, "Yeah, right. You wouldn't say that if you ever set foot inside of X church, attended Y political meeting, met my Z neighbor," and so on. I know. I'm with you. I can get really wound up when I see people who claim to be religious behaving in a way that indicates otherwise. I confess that my anger toward a certain person or a group of persons can get the better of me.

> The Christian ideal has not been tried and found wanting. It has been found difficult and left untried.
>
> —G. K. Chesterton, *What's Wrong with the World*

When that happens, I have enough training from attending Adult Children of Alcoholics (ACOA) and Al-Anon meetings in the '80s that I know I have to let go and let God. If I hold on to this negativity, then the resentment, anger, and bitterness will just eat me alive, thus making me unable to follow this amazingly difficult "love" commandment. I gotta forgive or I die. End of story.

I just finished reading a remarkable book, *Free of Charge: Giving and Forgiving in a Culture Stripped of Grace*, by Miroslav Volf. If you remember the excerpt of my interview with this theological thinker in Chapter Two, it's clear that this is not one of those New Age, feel-good books that teach us all how to live in "perfect harmony" and all that hooey. That kind of stuff gives me the willies. Rather, Volf gets down to the nitty-gritty of what it means for us as Christians to forgive those who have wronged us. Simply put, "We forgive because God forgives. We forgive as God forgives. We forgive by echoing God's forgiveness." While this is one of those deceptively simple lessons that takes me a minute to learn but a lifetime to master, Volf has given his fellow Christian brothers and sisters some tools to get us started on this journey toward reconciliation.

If you don't believe me, pick up a copy of the book and give it a shot. You have nothing to lose but your anger and resentment.

Lessons Learned from Billy Graham

But for those of us who are still kinda angry right now, I propose that we all take a break, have our milk and cookies, and see if we can learn a lesson in reconciliation from America's favorite evangelist, Billy Graham. When I covered his last crusade at Corona Park in Flushing Meadows, Queens, in June 2005, I learned that Jesus was not up on Capitol Hill making laws but right there standing beside each and every one of us.

These are the things I learned:

Share the Good News.

Be positive.

God is Love.

Preach so that people can find Him.

Practice what you proclaim.

You don't need mascara, prayer cloths, or a Holy Ghost machine gun to be an evangelist.

Say you're sorry when you make anti-Semitic comments.

Wash Franklin's mouth out with soap sometimes.

Pray.

Reading the Bible and praising the Lord are good for you.

Live a prayerful life—pray some and talk some and reflect and preach and play and write and work a little bit every day.

Talk to God every afternoon.

There are times when preachers can go too far in talking about social issues. Try to stick to the Gospel.

Be attuned to God. Remember the Clintons, for they are your friends; they love you, and you love them, and even though Billy Graham says he's a Democrat, most Republicans still love him.

Representatives and senators and Supreme Court justices and even the president in the White House—they all need Jesus. So do we.

And then remember the Gospel and the word that Jesus talked most about—the biggest problem of all—poverty.

In the words of my spiritual director Billy Joe Shaver, "If you don't love Jesus, you can go to hell."

–Kinky Friedman, musician, author, and Independent candidate for governor of Texas

Think what a better world it would be if we all took some time out for prayer and then gave each other a hug. Or if all ministers followed a basic policy to always practice what they preached and to say they're sorry sometimes.

And it is still true, no matter how old you are, when you get up to preach the Word, it is best to hold hands and love together. Amen.

Jesus Loves Me but He Can't Stand You

I know you smoke, I know you drink that brew
I just can't abide a sinner like you
God can't either, that's why I know it to be true that
Jesus loves me—but he can't stand you

I'm going to heaven, boys, when I die
'Cause I've crossed every "t" and I've dotted every "i"
My preacher tells me that I'm God's kind of guy; that's why
Jesus loves me—but you're gonna fry

God loves all his children, by gum
That don't mean he won't incinerate some
Can't you feel those hot flames licking you
Woo woo woo

I'm raising my kids in a righteous way
So don't be sending your kids over to my house to play
Yours'll grow up stoned, left-leaning, and gay; I know
Jesus told me on the phone today

Jesus loves me, this I know
And he told me where you're gonna go
There's lots of room for your kind down below
Whoa whoa whoa

Jesus loves me but he can't stand you . . .

12

JESUS LOVES ME,
THIS I KNOW

It is in our lives, and not from our words, that our
religion must be read.

—*Thomas Jefferson*

We've all heard the kiddie song that goes "Jesus loves me, this I know, for the Bible tells me so." While the words may be comforting, the song is usually sung in a Barney the dinosaur falsetto that makes most adults cringe, thus obscuring the powerful message behind these childlike lyrics.

But before we dismiss this seemingly simplistic saying outright, let's look at a reflection by the great German theologian Karl Barth. Even though he's penned such massive and influential theological tomes such as *Church Dogmatics*, his focus remained simple though by no means simplistic. At the core of his teachings was the belief that all knowledge comes through Christ, for He is God come to humanity. During his one trip to America in 1962, Barth was asked to summarize the main theme of his theology. The great theologian thought for a moment and replied: "Jesus loves me, this I know, for the Bible tells me so." If a serious German theologian like Barth can discover spiritual truth in this happy-happy joy-joy children's song, so can we. (And please, can we have a moratorium on those Protestant renditions of beloved hymns where all the singers look like they just ate too many prunes? I mean, is it the peace we're passing or . . . never mind.)

When I sat down to write this chapter, the smarty-pants side of me started to take over again. I found that I really needed a refresher course in Christ's love in the hope that I could get on the right track, more or less. So I picked up C. S. Lewis's book *The Four Loves*. Even though this book was written in 1960, like everything else this Oxford don wrote, it still inspires countless Christians today.

In *The Four Loves*, Lewis begins with affection (*storge*), or the love of the parent for his or her child. He then addresses the love of friendship (*philia*) and moves on to romantic love (*eros*). The final love (*agape*), which Lewis refers to as charity, represents the love between man and God. In the PBS documentary *The Question of God*, Peter Kreeft, a philosophy professor at Boston College, defines *agape*, as used in the New Testament, as "the love of God. The love that God has to us. And that love mediated and explained by Christ is absolutely egalitarian. Agape or charity is a scandal to reason because it means loving people not just in terms of justice or what they deserve, but simply loving them absolutely."

Steve Chalke, founder of the UK-based international outreach ministry Oasis, started a controversial firestorm when he came out with a book he wrote with Alan Mann, *The Lost Message of Jesus*, in which the authors chose to stress Jesus' unconditional love (*agape*) instead of God's wrathful judgment. Jim Wallis observes in *The Call to Conversion* that "the greatest need of our time is for *koinonia*, the call simply to be the church, to love one another, and to offer our lives for the sake of the world." I want to focus here on what our Christian communities would be like if we all bought into this agape deal. If we really believed that Jesus loved us unconditionally, then we'd be empowered to respond in kind.

In the farewell discourse in John, Jesus said, "If you love me, you will keep my commandments. And I will ask the Father, and he will give you another advocate to be with you forever. This is the Spirit of truth" (John 14:15–17a). Armed with this truth, we are transformed by the very grace of God that accepted us unconditionally. The Christian moral life begins with God's grace in Jesus Christ. As David Gushee and Dennis Hollinger point out in their essay "Toward an Evangelical Ethical Methodology," this grace "continues with the grateful response of a church that loves its Savior, a response of obedience that is directed and empowered by the Holy Spirit."

Yeah, I admit that this all sounds pretty radical. And yeah, this isn't what most churches these days look like. But when we look at the person of Jesus Christ, we see that He wasn't liberal or conservative. As I've stated before, He was a radical rule breaker and lovemaker, and that's what He is calling us to be as His disciples.

Aspiring to Be a Disciple

I know I am not there when it comes to following Christ. Heck, some days, I'm lucky if I can even find the path, which in my case can be as crooked and broken as all get-out. And I've experienced enough times in my life when there was only one set of footprints that I know in my heart that He will never give up on me. (For those of you unfamiliar with "Footprints in the Sand," it's a simple but profound poem penned by Mary Stevenson that describes a man walking with Jesus who notices two sets of footprints in the sand. He's puzzled because during times when he was really feeling desolate, there was only one set of footprints. Jesus says to him, "During your times of trial and suffering, when you see only one set of footprints, it was then that I carried you." And yes, it's schmaltzy, but I'm living proof that it's the truth. But once again, I digress.)

> The principle of transfiguration says nothing, no one and no situation, is "untransfigurable," that the whole of creation, nature, waits expectantly for its transfiguration, when it will be released from its bondage and share in the glorious liberty of the children of God, when it will not be just dry inert matter but will be translucent with divine glory.
> –Archbishop Desmond Tutu

Back to radical rule breakers like Jesus. I've known of at least one true radical in my lifetime—Martin Luther King Jr. He walked the walk when it came to living out the Beatitudes. King showed how we can love the sinner and not the sin. True radicals like King aren't afraid to call evil on the carpet and say something is sin when they see it, but they do so in the spirit of brotherly love and nonviolent protest.

Real radicals like King, Catholic Worker movement founder Dorothy Day, and antiwar activist Philip Berrigan aren't afraid of Jesus because they know that adhering to Christ's teachings of nonviolent love, regardless of the cost, is what's required of those who dare call themselves "disciples of Christ." Based on their collective writings, these followers of Christ appeared to have found considerable strength in knowing that despite their human failings, they were able to critique the sin and not the sinner in such a way that Christ's love shone through. Just look at what they were able to do.

Chalke and Mann ask these challenging questions: "To what extent does the Church model the spiritually and socially inclusive message of Jesus? Are we liberators of excluded people or simply another dimension of their oppression? We may not exclude tax-collectors or hemorrhaging women, but what about schizophrenics, divorcees, single people, one-parent families, drug users, transsexuals or those struggling with their faith?" To this list I would add Christians we see as our political adversaries.

When we put partisan politics above seeking the Kingdom of God, we get what we deserve. Mike Yaconelli reflected, "The impotence of today's Church, the weakness of Christ's followers, and the irrelevance of most parachurch organizations is directly related to the lack of being in the presence of an awesome, holy God, who continually demands allegiance only to Him—not to our organizations, to our churches or our theology."

The Sojourners' slogan has it right: God is not a Democrat or a Republican but rather Lord of all. And as Christians, it is our duty to let His light shine through instead of trying to advance our own personal and at times petty sociopolitical agendas.

As Christians, we are called to be the salt of the world, but when we fail to follow Him, we're just dishing out Christ's teachings sans any seasoning (see Matthew 5:13). As Chalke and Mann note, "We get the Christianity we deserve—*we just can't pass the buck.* The Church in the West—with some notable exceptions—has a tame faith because it has been giving a tame message for centuries. You can't breed a radical, revolutionary movement on passive, middle-of-the-road rhetoric."

Stanley Hauerwas notes that "Christians' first political responsibility is to be the church, and by being the church, they should understand that their first loyalty is to God, the God we worship as Christians, in a manner that understands that we are not first and foremost about making democracy work, but about the truthful worship of the true God." The challenge I present to U.S. churches is to seek to create the type of worshiping communities where red and blue Christians can come together not as political rivals seeking to do battle but in communion, joined together through baptism as brothers and sisters in Christ.

Church in Action

I know this is difficult, but I've witnessed firsthand a few examples of inclusive Christian communities in action. Also, through my work with *The Wittenburg Door*, I have become aware of other such gatherings. Most of these groups, though, do seem to exist on the fringes of the denominational hierarchy as they live out the Gospel while flying under the radar, so to speak. Unfortunately, when I've seen these groups grow in size and become a vocal witness, the Religious Right and PC police tend to step in and try to shut down the party. Now, granted, we're not in a situation like the early church, where similar gatherings were illegal. Anyone who thinks Christians have it bad now would do well to take a quick review of church history, as there have been times when being identified as a Christian would get you killed (see Appendix B for a quick recap of infamous dates in church history). I'll take a good mocking over a flaying any day of the week. It's that old sticks-and-stones analogy, you know.

For now at least, I've found a spiritual home in the emerging church movement. After the 2004 election, my quest for a church community took me to a small service on the Upper East Side of Manhattan. I was shocked that I could praise God without having

My most consistent prayer now is, "Dear God, keep me from doing anything as if I were on my own. Please don't let me forget that you are always with me."

    —Gerald May, "The Vision and the Path"

to pledge my allegiance to a particular political party. At this alternative worship service, called, appropriately, Sanctuary, the music and the beauty of the liturgy draw us into communion with God. As the church's Web site notes, "This service is an evolving endeavor to translate two thousand years of Christian tradition into the language we speak today: the fast-paced, multi-faceted, urban language of New York." It strives to be a church "where people worship as whole beings; as they refuse to limit their minds, stifle their spirits, or still their bodies. And yet, they revel in all that tradition has to give the Christian community: bread and wine, incense and chant, and the story of Jesus as savior and healer in scripture."

I leave these services having been loved by Jesus and empowered to try to follow His teachings. What I love most about these services is that I have no clue how most of these people vote, and frankly, I don't care. I'd rather focus on their prayerful and faithful presence, which enables us to be the church in the world.

Now, before you start throwing your 1928 *Book of Common Prayer* at me, I know that there are people who like things to be a lot more traditional than I do—and that's fantastic. Jesus doesn't care one bit if you prefer to worship God with stately organ music, the strums of an acoustic guitar, the sounds of hip-hop emanating from da Bronx, a heavy rock beat, or even total silence. Let's face it, if we all thought and worshiped the same way, the Christian community would be one gigantic, boring snoozefest. We need to talk to God in the language that works for us—just as on the day of Pentecost (see Acts 2:2–4). By praying together the prayer that Jesus gave us, in our preferred God-talk, we allow the words of the Lord's Prayer to touch our hearts (see Matthew 6:9–13). The more we let His will be done, the better able we will be to allow the love of Christ to transform us into the kind of Christians He intended us to be. Thanks be to God.

Epilogue:
Where Do We Go from Here?

> Every day people are straying away from the church
> and going back to God.
> —*Lenny Bruce, "Christ and Moses"*

In southern author Flannery O'Connor's novel *Wise Blood*, Hazel Motes gets so frustrated with Christian hypocrites that he forms his own "Church of Christ Without Christ." Motes describes this church as peaceful and satisfied—a place where the lame don't walk, the blind don't see, and what's dead stays that way. When we as Christians go against the teachings of Christ, we create such a church—a sanctuary that's devoid of any power to live out the transformative message of the Gospel. And like Motes, we end up dead and blind and found wandering around aimlessly along some seemingly deserted road.

But John Dear, a Jesuit priest and peace activist, notes:

Just because the culture and the cultural church have now joined with the empire and its wars does not mean that we all have to go along with such heresy, or fall into despair as if nothing can be done. It is never too late to follow the troublemaking Jesus, to join his practice of revolutionary nonviolence and become authentic Christians. We may find ourselves in trouble, even at the hands of so-called Christians, just as Jesus was in trouble at the hands of the so-called religious leaders of his day. But this very trouble may lead us back to those Beatitude blessings.

As God gave us free will, we have two choices. We can do what too many Christians do, which is pick and choose those passages of Scripture that we find pleasing to our eyes and ignore the bits of the Bible that we feel don't really apply to us. But as Flannery O'Connor illustrates, when we turn our backs on His word, we end up living a life that may look OK on the surface, but when we peel away the slick veneer, we see that we've become devoid of any real meaning or substance.

Our second option is to try to live out the teachings of Christ knowing full well that following the Gospel to the fullest will get us into trouble. A lot of trouble. Show me one true-blue disciple of Christ who had an easy time of it once he or she picked up the cross and really followed Jesus' teachings.

Lest anyone think that making the changes I've suggested in the preceding pages is are truly impossible, let's not forget the dilemma Paul was preoccupied with in the Epistles, which was the problem of bringing together two deeply separated and bitterly distrustful groups—the Jews and the Gentiles—into one community. Despite the sociopolitical climate, which should have doomed such a massive and idealistic undertaking, Paul and his peers succeeded, and they did so to such a degree that the Way of Christ spread like wildfire among the Gentiles.

> People feel a near-desperate desire to reconnect to the sacred, to find some way to unite their lives with a higher meaning and purpose and in particular to that aspect of the sacred that is built on the loving, kind and generous energy in the universe.
>
> —Michael Lerner, *The Left Hand of God*

Recently, I've received a slew of e-mails about the Network of Spiritual Progressives, a community of people from many faiths and traditions, called together by *Tikkun* magazine and its vision of healing and transforming our world. Time will tell if this group, which includes in this call both the outer transformation needed to achieve social justice, ecological sanity, and world peace and the inner healing needed to foster loving relationships, will develop into a true ecumenical body of believers that will welcome all spiritual seekers (including Republicans), but the early signs look very promising. If I sound skeptical, it's because I know Christians who would support this group's mission, but the words *liberal* and *progressive* turn them off. So I pray that we can find creative ways to look beyond labels as we all seek to remain faithful witnesses to Christ.

Also, I am getting some really interesting e-mails from groups like Emergent Village, Sojo.net, and Greenbelt (UK). In addition, I've been receiving resource material like "For the Peace of the World: A Christian Curriculum on International Relations," put out by the National Council of Churches of Christ USA, and information about peace initiatives such as the UN International Day of Peace, celebrated each year on September 21. So something is brewing here, and I pray that we can all smell the coffee and wake up ready and rarin' to go.

In the end, will we as a Christian community dare to let the radical love of Christ reign supreme? I pray to God the answer is yes.

> I suggest first that all of you Christians, missionaries and all, must begin to live more like Jesus Christ. Second, I would suggest that you must practice your religion without adulterating it or toning it down. Third, I would suggest that you must put your emphasis on love, for love is the center and soul in Christianity. Fourth, I would suggest that you study the non-Christian religions more sympathetically in order to find the good that is in them, so that you might have a more sympathetic approach to the people.
>
> —Mahatma Gandhi, *Christ of the Indian Road*

Appendix A
Unholy Scripture

This is the prophecy (originally published as "The Revelation of Dubya") that was foretold in the July-August 2001 issue of *The Wittenburg Door* following the November 2000 selection of George W. Bush to the presidency. Although John Ashcroft and a few other players have left the scene since then, this prophecy continues to unfold. As this is a prophecy in progress, this revelation should be taken as prophetic signs of things to come rather than a fact-based report.

The Revelation of Dubya

1 The Revelation of the burning Bush, which will show what soon must take place; the Bush Klan made their will known by giving the presidency to I, the Dubya, 2 who will conform my administration to my Father's likeness and image. 3 Blessed am I, the Dubya, who obeys my Father's will on behalf of the Bush Klan, and blessed are my fundraisers, and blessed are those who are white, male, and Republican, for their time is here.

Prayer to the Faithful

4 I, Dubya, pray to the followers who gave me the election. I'm a uniter not a divider; 5 for you see, my enemies misunderestimated me. As I build a strategoric Bush Klan, I seek to unite both Democrat and Republican until everyone believes that I am a compassionate conservative; 6 and I will execute those who mention my drunk driving arrest and history of drug use, for I sobered up by my fortieth

birthday. 7Lo! I, the Dubya, the savior of the Religious Right, have armed myself with Promise Keepers, 8every woman will adore these godly men, even those who used to be feminists; and on my accounts the Democrats will never be elected again. 9So it is to be. Yee-haw!

The Believer in Politics

10   "I am pro-life, pro-family and pro-Republican," so said my Father to me. 11And he commanded me to establish his vision for America, which will replace the evil laws of the Democrats. For once Americans are living under a Bush, I can use my experience with Arbusto (that's Spanish for Bush) Energy, Inc., to exploit our nation's natural riches. 12Therefore, multinational oil and gas companies can continue to back the Bush Klan and their funds will enrich my reelection campaign.

13   To build my self-righteous kingdom, the faithful will be divided into the Seven Tribes of Dubya: the National Rifle Association, American Family Association, Focus on the Family, Christian Coalition, Concerned Women for America, Council for National Policy, and National Right to Life Committee. 14These self-appointed leaders of the fire-breathing Religious Right are eager to do my bidding and profit from my position as leader of the most powerful nation in the world. 15I have commanded these tribes to recruit others, who will recruit others and so on and so on until I, the Dubya, rule the nation, prospering greatly at the expense of everyone. 16To these inerrant believers, I say:

To the National Rifle Association

2 To NRA President Charlton Heston: "You are a great man for leading God's chosen people out of the wilderness to the promised land. For in *The Ten Commandments*, God spoke to you through my ancestor the original burning Bush. 2I also know that you stood up for the white man in *Planet of the Apes*. 3After eight years of an aggressive antigun administration, with your leadership,

we will restore Second Amendment rights to all Americans or die fighting the battle."

To Focus on the Family

4   And to Dr. James Dobson of Focus on the Family: "I applaud you for your cleverness in disguising yourself as a caring and nurturing child psychologist, when in fact, you are a fierce pro-family political fighter. 5Because I think you called John Ashcroft 'a clear boon to the pro-family movement,' you have proved yourself to be a loyal and faithful servant. 6Whenever the liberal heathens picket Colorado and slander your holy name, stand firm, for I am now Commander-in-Chief and will use any means at my disposal to defend our version of family values."

To the American Family Association

7   And to Don Wildmon of the American Family Association: "I counsel you to continue your holy crusades to rid the world of NEA and PBS-funded pornography. 8Behold, John Ashcroft and I are standing at the door knocking, for we desire to share in the fruits of your raids. 9To him who shares in the pornography gathered from his harvest, I will grant a place with me on the throne. 10However, for those who will not let other godly leaders sample their offerings, they will be cast into the darkness and turned over to the Feminazis."

To the Christian Coalition

11   And to Pat Robertson of the Christian Coalition: "I know your works, your lobbying, and political savvy. 12But I have this against you: without Ralph Reed, your organization could not galvanize the Religious Right in a manner that is pleasing to my eye. 13Furthermore, you were unable to keep Pat Buchanan in your fold, thus causing me a loss of votes among my devoted followers in Christian Identity, the Army of God, and other Bible-believing warriors. 14For the sake of

my self-righteousness agenda, reestablish the Christian Coalition to its former glory and I will reward you when I come."

To Concerned Women of America

3 And to Beverly LaHaye of Concerned Women for America: "You have fought hard for your God-given right to be submissive to men. [2] I thank you for telling the liberals that I have the God-given right to make my cabinet as conservative as I want. [3] Now, we are coming some day; hold fast to what you have, so that only a true believer may seize your prize. I bless your group for your heavenly smiles and your hair that praises Jesus. [4] May the National Organization of Women and all other feminists hear what my Spirit is saying through these heavenly bodies."

To the Council for National Policy

5   And to Tim LaHaye of the Council for National Policy: "I delight in your holy crusade to unite our nation's richest pro-life warriors, Second Amendment crusaders, antitax advocates, financiers, and politicians in our quest to Christianize America. [6] As I think I heard my faithful servant Ollie North say, 'The kinds of people that are involved in this organization reflect the best of what America is.' [7] Continue to clothe our organization's whereabouts in secrecy, so that together we can safeguard our righteous agenda from distortion by those Democratic demons, who seek to expose and destroy our sacred mission."

To the National Right to Life Committee

8   And to Wanda Franz of the National Right to Life Committee: "I applaud your work in aborting the efforts of those who unjustly tried to block the nomination of John Ashcroft for attorney general. [9] Together, we can kill any pro-choice legislation, leading the way so we can someday soon overturn *Roe* v. *Wade*. [10] With

your advisement, I would like to craft legislation that will make baby killings a capital crime, thereby allowing me to execute abortion doctors for their heinous acts."

The Road to Victory

4 As America entered the new millennium, I, the Dubya, was anointed to lead the Republicans to Victory! 2As I stood before the 2000 Republican Convention, I could feel the Log Cabin Republicans and the Religious Right coming together until we all thought like one.

3   Then I saw John McCain and other wayward Republicans joining forces with me to push for my godly agenda. 4And I saw gathering at my feet the inerrant followers of the Seven Tribes of Dubya: 5the National Rifle Association, Focus on the Family, the American Family Association, the Christian Coalition, Concerned Women of America, the Council of National Policy, and the National Right to Life Committee; 6all faithful followers willing to serve according to my self-righteous desires. 7As these members recruit additional members, the burning Bush will continue to light up the world.

8   On November 8, I saw the emergence of the seven minor pseudoprophets, Florida Secretary of State Katherine Harris, Florida Governor Jeb Bush, Justice O'Connor, Justice Rehnquist, Justice Scalia, Justice Thomas, and Justice Kennedy. 9Though small in number, these pseudoprophets proved invaluable in safeguarding my position as President. 10And to help me grow financially, I am indebted to seven moneychangers: Louis A. Beecherl Jr., owner, Beecherl Investments; Sam Fox, CEO and chair, Harbour Group; Richard and Nancy Kinder, chair and CEO, Kinder Morgan Energy Partners; Kenneth Lay, chair and CEO, Enron Corp.; Tom and Nancy Loeffler, lobbyists, Arter & Hadden; John N. Palmer Sr., chair, GulfSouth Capital, Inc.; and Alex G. Spanos, chair, A. G. Spanos Companies; 11as well as the more than two hundred other Pioneer donors, without whom I could not have stolen this election.

12   Next, I had a vision, where I saw a great multitude of Republicans from across the state of Florida casting aside all ballots with hanging, pregnant, or indented chads. 13They are crying out in a loud voice, "I have seen the light of the burning Bush, and I will not let Al Gore win!" 14The U.S. Supreme Court heard their cries and anointed me the 43rd President of the United States.

15   As President of this great nation, I nominated John Ashcroft to be my attorney general and Gale Norton as my interior secretary; 16these appointments mean that my claim to be a compassionate conservative was a campaign slogan used to conceal my true pro-life, anti–civil rights, and antienvironment agenda. 17Also, I set up an office to coordinate faith-based and community initiatives, though the true purpose of this group is known only to those who are true-blue blood Bush backers.

18   And many of the Democrats, each of them with no backbone, met with me in the White House. 19They approved Ashcroft and Norton without question, saying, "We want full bipartisan leadership; therefore, we will serve you, Dubya, and vote according to your commands."

The Democratic Beast

5 And I saw the Democratic beast named Al Gore coming out of the Florida swamps having won the popular vote but lost the presidential election in the Electoral College. 2The Gore beast opened its mouth to utter falsehoods against the Bushes, blaspheming my family name and my Father's policies. 3Also, this beast was allowed to raise money in a Buddhist temple despite my prayerful pleas that only Republicans can raise money in religious dwellings. 4Furthermore, this Vietnam veteran spewed lies against my military record, calling me a draft dodger despite my stateside service in the Texas Air Guard. 5To my delight, the Democratic Party leaders devoured this beast and his cries were silenced.

6   Then I saw the beast called Clinton that rose up next to this dead Gore beast; it was destroying White House property and par-

doning criminals. 7The Clinton beast took away all the limelight away from the Gore beast, for the Clinton beast was more popular with the media. 8However, as the Clinton beast had ruled for eight years, his power has now diminished greatly. 9Now the Hillary beast has emerged to replace the Clinton beast, though the Republican leadership has vowed to rob the Hillary beast of all her elected power.

10   At first, I was fearful of these two beasts, for their pseudo-liberal polices were almost identical to my self-righteous agenda. 11However, I heard the word of the Lord say to me, Fear not, Dubya, for these beasts have ended their reign. 12In the year of our Lord two thousand and one, I have preordained that you will assume your rightful place as ruler of the Promised Land that I have called Washington, D.C.

The New Jerusalem

6 Then I, the Dubya, saw a bipartisan Congress with me as President, for the Democrats' brand of pseudoliberalism had passed away, and the Clinton and Gore beasts were no more. 2As I climbed up the steps of my nation's capitol, I saw the land that was now mine. 3Joining me in this journey to the Promised Land are the Seven Tribes of Dubya and their legion of inerrant followers, the seven minor pseudoprophets, the seven moneychangers, and the Pioneer donors, as well as those members of Congress, who agreed to cast their votes according to the will of the Bush Klan.

4   In this New Jerusalem, there will be no need of any social program begun by Democratic heathens, 5and with my Father as my guiding light; the burning Bush will shine over this great nation. 6For my Father, the God of the Republican faithful, has sent me, the Dubya, as his Son to show his servants what must soon take place. 7See, I am coming soon! Blessed are those who obey my words without thinking. 8Soon everyone will be converted to my beliefs and our nation will prosper under the Republican authority of a godly white male leadership. 9Blessed are those who believe in

me and give me money, for without soft money, the Bush Klan cannot prosper. [10]Yes, my fellow believers, the time has come for the Bush Klan to rule the world, bringing our version of the Gospel into every home in America. [11]Thanks to my family's blessed connections with Skull and Bones and the CIA. I, the Dubya, with the help of my Father, can promise that the burning Bush will remain lit for all eternity. [12]Yee-haw! Thanks be to my family.

The DNC Response

We regret that the Democratic National Committee is unable to respond to any requests for information, analysis, or misinterpretation. Furthermore, we cannot at this time throw any publicly televised hissy fits, temper tantrums, or general outbursts. At the present time, we are conducting unscientific experiments to ascertain how fast we have to drink our Slurpees in order to get a really good collective brain freeze.

Have a Good Day. Don't Worry, Be Happy. And of course, Smile!

Appendix B
Selected Dates
in Christian History

A.D. 1   First year in the Christian calendar. (Later, monks working in the dark ended up miscalculating the date just a bit. It turns out that Jesus was somewhere between 4 and 8 years old in year 1.)

29 to 33   Jesus is executed in Jerusalem.

33   Stephen is stoned, thus becoming the first Christian martyr.

62   Paul is martyred in Rome for treason.

64   Great fire in Rome, started by Emperor Nero, is blamed on the Christians.

313   Edict of Milan establishes toleration of Christianity. Persecutions continue to the present day.

325   Council of Nicaea adopts the Nicene Creed.

394   Christianity becomes the official religion of the Roman Empire.

587   Visigoths of Spain are converted to Christianity.

596   Saint Augustine of Canterbury is sent to convert Britain to Christianity.

1054   Split between the Eastern and Western churches is formalized. There goes the neighborhood.

1095–1291 The Crusades

1274   Thomas Aquinas, theologian and philosopher, dies a reasonable death.

1380–1382	John Wycliffe translates the Bible into English and expresses unorthodox views of the sacraments (Penance and the Eucharist), the use of relics, and celibacy of the clergy.
1431	Joan of Arc is martyred, thereby providing a really juicy acting role later on for leading ladies like Ingrid Bergman, Jean Seberg, and Leelee Sobieski.
1478	Pope Sixtus IV establishes the Spanish Inquisition. Nobody expected it.
1494–1497	Leonardo da Vinci paints *The Last Supper*.
1509–1512	Michelangelo paints the ceiling of the Sistine Chapel in Rome.
1517	Martin Luther nails the Catholic Church by posting his Ninety-Five Theses on the door of the Wittenberg cathedral. There is nothing pretty about this picture.
1534	Henry VIII tells the pope to MYOB and prompts the establishment of the Anglican (Episcopal) Church.
1536	John Calvin publishes *The Institutes of the Christian Religion*, a book predestined for success.
1609	Baptist Church is founded by John Smyth, leading to an immediate ban on dancing, drinking, and gambling.
1636	Roger Williams founds Rhode Island to welcome religious dissenters after having been banished by the Puritans from Massachusetts.
1692	Salem Witch trials begin.
1739	Methodist Church is founded by John Wesley.
1741	Jonathan Edwards preaches his infamous sermon "Sinners in the Hand of an Angry God." America is now wide awake.

1802	Thomas Jefferson coins the phrase "a wall of separation between church and state."
1820s–1830s	Second Great Awakening. Here we go again and again and again and again.
1878	Fourteen-point creed of the Niagara Bible Conference is approved and immediately adopted by fundamentalists. There goes the Enlightenment.
1882	Nietzsche declares, "God is dead."
1899	Carrie Nation raids and wrecks a saloon in Medicine Lodge, Kansas, the first of many she'll hit. I won't drink to that.
1900	God declares, "Nietzsche is dead."
1915	Former Methodist minister William J. Simmons revitalizes the Ku Klux Klan and introduces the practice of cross-burning.
1925	Scopes Monkey Trial causes devolution among fundamentalists.
1926	Evangelist Aimee Semple McPherson disappears and reappears, leading to a trial for fraud.
1927	Bob Jones University is founded.
1930	Marion Gordon "Pat" Robertson is born, proving once and for all he is not "divinely inspired."
1934	Billy Graham makes a personal commitment to Christ through the ministry of Mordecai Ham, a traveling evangelist.
1942	National Association of Evangelicals is founded. Fundamentalists are furious.
1945	Hiroshima happens.
1948	World Council of Churches is founded. Fundamentalists are really furious.

1949	Dead Sea Scrolls are discovered.
1952	Norman Vincent Peale writes *The Power of Positive Thinking*.
1954	Army-McCarthy hearings demonstrate the power of paranoia.
1956	*The Ten Commandments* is released as a major motion picture, starring Charlton Heston as Moses.
1960	*Elmer Gantry* is released as a major motion picture. Praise the Lord and pass the offering plate.
1960	Madalyn Murray (later O'Hair) raises holy hell about prayer in the schools.
1960	John Fitzgerald Kennedy is elected first Catholic president. The pope is pleased.
1961	CBN radio and TV goes on the air for the first time.
1961	James Orsen Bakker marries Tammy Faye LaValley. Maybelline stock soars.
1962–1965	Second Vatican Council. Catholics start doing "The Vatican Rag."
1963	Charlton (Moses) Heston joins Marlon Brando and Martin Luther King Jr. in the March on Washington.
1965	*The Greatest Story Ever Told* is released as a major motion picture, starring Charlton Heston as John the Baptist.
1966	John Lennon declares the Beatles more popular than Jesus.
1967	James Dobson earns his Ph.D. from the University of Southern California in the field of child development.
1968	*Rosemary's Baby* is released.
1968	Death of God movement dies.

1971	Billy James Hargis founds American Christian College but has to resign shortly thereafter upon admitting that he had sex with young male college students.
1971	First issue of *The Wittenburg Door* is published.
1971	The rock opera *Jesus Christ Superstar* debuts, setting the stage for a string of god-awful Andrew Lloyd Webber Broadway musicals.
1973	Trinity Broadcasting Network goes on the air. Kmart reports a nationwide shortage of AquaNet.
1974	The Philadelphia Eleven chicks prove that each of them can be one of the boys when they become the first ordained female Episcopal priests, a move that causes many a stiff upper lip to quiver.
1974	*PTL Club* goes on the air begging for bread.
1974	Bread for the World is founded.
1976	Habitat for Humanity is founded.
1979	Paige Patterson and Paul Pressler plan a coup d'état of the Southern Baptist Convention over black coffee and beignets at the Café du Monde in New Orleans.
1979	Monty Python's *Life of Brian* encourages Christians to "always look on the bright side of life."
1979	Jerry Falwell sees nothing but doom and gloom ahead because Jimmy Carter clearly isn't the right kind of Christian to be president. Falwell founds the Moral Majority. Jesus announces he's now in the minority.
1981	Supersecret Council for National Policy is founded by Tim LaHaye. Shhhh—don't tell anyone.
1987	Oral Roberts claims that God will "call him home" if he is unable to raise $8 million. God tells Oral there's no room in heaven, so Oral is stuck here on earth.
1987	Jim Bakker admits to adultery; resigns from the PTL.

1987	Pat Robertson announces that God has anointed him to be president despite the Almighty's protestations to the contrary.
1987	Episcopal Bishop John Shelby Spong ordains Robert Williams, an openly gay priest, only to defrock him a few months later when Williams says Mother Teresa should "get laid."
1988	Jimmy Swaggart admits to pornographic activities; his ministry falls apart.
1988	Berlin Wall comes tumbling down.
1989	Andres Serrano creates a sensation when he photographs a crucifix submerged in a glass bottle of the artist's urine and calls it "art."
1989	Religious Right leaders demand that the National Endowment for the Arts (NEA) stop funding pornographic, anti-Christian works of art; encourage instead the funding of crucifix mobiles made during Vacation Bible School.
1991	Former University of Colorado football coach Bill McCartney throws a Hail Mary pass and founds the Promise Keepers.
1991	*Primetime Live* and Trinity Foundation expose Robert Tilton's ministry.
1992	Bishop Spong outs the Apostle Paul in his book *Rescuing the Bible from Fundamentalism*.
1993	U.S. Catholic Church caught with its pants down as pedophile priests are exposed.
1995	President Bill Clinton has a spiritual awakening according to Dick Morris, Fox News commentator and former political adviser to Clinton.
1996	*The Wittenburg Door* is pulled from Christian bookstores by Spring Arbor Distributors for naming Beavis and Butt-head "Theologians of the Decade."

1996	The Center for Reclaiming America is founded by D. James Kennedy as an outreach of Coral Ridge Ministries to mobilize Christians at the grassroots level.
1996	Federal Elections Commission files suit against the Christian Coalition, claiming it acted illegally by promoting Republican candidates in 1990, '92, and '94.
1996	Ellen Cooke, former treasurer of the Episcopal Church, is sentenced to five years in prison for embezzling over $2 million.
1996	Nine hundred women "savor the life-giving juices of their bodies and the planet" as they praise the goddess Sophia through a milk 'n' honey Eucharist; father church is not amused.
1996	Mother Teresa's sweet likeness is spotted on a sticky bun.
1997	Southern Baptist Convention votes to boycott Disney.
1997	Mr. Hankey, the Christmas Poo, reunites the war-ring Jewish and Christian factions in *South Park*.
1998	Charlton Heston, a.k.a. Moses, packs heat as president of the NRA.
1998	Jesus and Satan fight a battle for spiritual domination on *South Park*.
1998	Southern Baptist Convention votes for wives to graciously submit to their husbands.
1998	President Clinton is caught with his pants down, but in the end, it's the Religious Right's butt boy Kenneth Starr who's exposed.
2000	Despite Pat Robertson's prayerful protestations, the Y2K bug fails to end life as we know it.

2001	Lawsuits start flying in an effort to remove a Ten Commandments monument from an Alabama courthouse.
2001	National Religious Broadcasters pulls the plug on its fifty-seven-year relationship with the National Association of Evangelicals.
2003	Gene Robinson becomes first openly gay bishop in the Episcopal Church, leading to a three-year suspension from the mother church.
2003	*The da Vinci Code* and *Armageddon* become controversial best-sellers, with too many Christians taking these works of fiction way too seriously.
2004	Even though God is not a Democrat or a Republican, the Religious Right anoints George W. Bush as God's choice to lead the United States, hereafter known as the Promised Land. The Lord is not particularly pleased.
2004	Mel Gibson mass markets *The Passion of the Christ*, proving that even in "Hellywood," a person can be a believer and still bring in the bucks.
2005	National Clergy Council president Rob Schenck storms out of the Billy Graham Crusade after witnessing a love fest between Bill and Hillary Clinton and Graham.
2008	DNC rediscovers its moral backbone and assumes control of the White House.
2012	DNC loses its moral backbone thanks to yet another intern scandal. RNC reassumes control of the White House.
2664	DNC finds ancient missing moral backbone, assumes control of the White House and Congress.
2666	Hell freezes over.

Appendix C
For Further Reflection

Here are some Web sites that I've found to be helpful in my spiritual journey of sorts. As in the case of a twelve-step meeting, take what works for you and leave the rest. Godspeed and Peace.

Where I Reflect

Beliefnet:
http://www.beliefnet.com

CT Direct Daily headlines, commentary, and site news from *Christianity Today* magazine:
http://www.ChristianityToday.com

Evangelicals for Social Action:
http://www.esa-online.org

International Day of Peace—September 21:
http://www.internationaldayofpeace.org

Joan Chittister's Weekly "From Where I Stand" column:
http://nationalcatholicreporter.org/fwis/index.htm

The Revealer:
http://www.therevealer.org

Sojourners:
http://www.sojo.net

SoMA: A Review of Religion and Culture—Society of Mutual Autopsy:

http://www.somareview.com

Where I Laugh

Mrs. Betty Bowers, America's Best Christian:

http://www.bettybowers.com

The Daily Show:

http://www.comedycentral.com/tv_shows/ thedailyshowwithjonstewart

Landover Baptist Church:

http://www.landoverbaptist.org

The Onion:

http://www.theonion.com

Presidential Prayer Team:

http://www.presidentialprayerteam.org

Ship of Fools:

http://www.ship-of-fools.com

The Wittenburg Door:

http://www.wittenburgdoor.com

Where I Pray

Emergent Village:

http://www.emergentvillage.com

Greenbelt:

http://www.greenbelt.org.uk

Henri Nouwen Society:

http://www.henrinouwen.org

Sanctuary:

www.sanctuaryny.org

References

Preface

Jonathan Swift's observation is taken from his essay "Thoughts on Various Subjects, Moral and Diverting," written in 1706 and published in *The Works of Jonathan Swift* (New York: Derby & Jackson, 1860), p. 608.

Introduction

The Landover Baptist Church's bumper sticker can be found at http://www.cafepress.com/landoverbaptist/52680.

Justice Potter Stewart made his comment in a concurring opinion accompanying the 6–3 ruling that overturned a ban on pornographic films, June 22, 1964.

The George Washington quotation is from a letter he wrote to Sir Edward Newenham on June 22, 1792.

Jerry Falwell's comment about reelecting President Bush appeared in his e-mail newsletter, *Falwell Confidential*, July 1, 2004, and on his Web site, http://falwell.com.

Jon Stewart's comment was made during an interview with Bill Moyers on *NOW* (Public Broadcasting System) on July 12, 2003; the transcript is posted at http://www.pbs.org/now/transcript/transcript_stewart.html.

Call to Renewal's 2004 election ad campaign can be found on the organization's Web site at http://www.sojo.net/index.cfm?action=action.election&item=petition_flash.

The United Methodist Church's statement is from Marta W. Aldrich, "Beyond Red, Blue: The Church as Post-Election Healer," posted December 21, 2004, at http://archives.umc.org/interior .asp?mid=6301.

The quote by Tony Campolo is from his book *Speaking My Mind* (Nashville, Tenn.: W Publishing Group, 2005), p. 134.

Anne Lamott was quoted in an interview by Wendy Schuman, "Anne Lamott: 'God's in the Struggle with Us,'" originally published by Beliefnet on May 22, 2005, at http://www.beliefnet.com/ story/167/story_16714_1.html.

Chapter One

The Stan Marsh quote is from *South Park*, season 8, episode 3, "The Passion of the Jew," first broadcast on March 31, 2004.

John W. Whitehead's comment is from "Churches and the Corrupting Influence of Politics," posted July 26, 2004, on the Web site of the Rutherford Institute at http://www.rutherford.org/articles_db/ commentary.asp?record_id=292.

Brian McLaren's observation is from *A Generous Orthodoxy* (Grand Rapids, Mich.: Zondervan, 2004), p. 70.

Mark Twain's quote is from *Letters from the Earth: Uncensored Writings* (New York: HarperCollins, 1962), p. 237.

Pat Robertson's "Perspective on the Greatest Commandment" can be found at CBN.com at http://www.cbn.com/spirituallife/ BibleStudyAndTheology/Perspectives/Pat_Greatest_Commandment .asp. On the Hugo Chavez incident, see "Robertson Apologizes for Assassination Call," posted on August 24, 2005, on CNN.com at http://www.cnn.com/2005/US/08/24/robertson.chavez, and "Pat Robertson Clarifies His Statement Regarding Hugo Chavez" posted on the same date on CBN.com at http://www.patrobertson.com/ pressreleases/hugochavez.asp. His comment about nuking the State Department is documented in "Pat Robertson's 'Nuke' Idea Draws Protest," posted on October 9, 2003, on CNN.com at http://www .cnn.com/2003/US/10/09/robertson.state.

Greg Palast's estimate of Robertson's net worth and Robertson's Antichrist quote are from "I Don't Have to Be Nice to the Spirit of the Antichrist," published in the London *Observer* on May 23, 1999. It is reprinted at http://www.guardian.co.uk/Archive/Article/0,4273,3867951,00.html.

Robertson's "quest" is noted in Daniel Roth, "Pat Robertson's Quest for Eternal Life," *Fortune*, May 28, 2002. Robertson's book, *The New World Order* (Nashville, Tenn.: W Publishing Group), was published in 2002.

Ron Sider's quote is from an interview with Stan Guthrie titled "The Evangelical Scandal" that appeared in *Christianity Today* on April 27, 1992; it can be read at http://www.christianitytoday.com/ct/2005/004/32.70.html.

The National Association of Evangelicals' position paper "For the Health of the Nation" (adopted October 7, 2004) can be found at http://www.nae.net/images/civic_responsibility2.pdf; the quotation is from page 4. The list of signers of this document are listed on the MSNBC Web site; see "Evangelicals Rethink Their Public Face," posted May 23, 2005, at http://msnbc.msn.com/id/7911488.

Information about the 2004 conference titled "Examining the Real Agenda of the Religious Far Right" can be found at http://www.opencenter.org/Trainings/Religious_Right_Agenda.html.

Information about the Faith and Politics Institute can be found at http://www.faithandpolitics.org.

The Dalai Lama's words are from "The Global Community and the Need for Universal Responsibility" at http://www.purifymind.com/GlobalComm.htm.

Dr. Martin Luther King Jr.'s "Loving Your Enemies" can be found at http://www.stanford.edu/group/King/sermons/571117.002_Loving_Your_Enemies.html.

The comment by Candace Chellew-Hodge is from "What's So Funny 'bout Peace, Love, and Understanding?" at http://www.whosoever.org/v9i6/peace.shtml.

Jimmy Carter's comment is from his book *Our Endangered Values: America's Moral Crisis* (New York: Simon & Schuster, 2005), p. 185.

The quote from Thich Nhat Hanh is from *Taming the Tiger Within* (New York: Riverhead Books, 2005), p. 273.

Chapter Two

Father Mychal Judge died in the World Trade Center terrorist attack on September 11, 2001. His poem is copyright © 2001 by the Franciscans Holy Name Province and is reprinted with their permission. Every year, on the Sunday before the 9/11 anniversary, the FDNY Fire Family Transport Foundation and NYPD detective Steven McDonald cosponsor the Mychal Judge Walk of Remembrance to honor the 343 rescue workers who were lost on that day and to celebrate the legacy of Father Judge's ministry.

Father James Martin's observations are from his interview in *The Wittenburg Door* for September-October 2002, pp. 12–19.

Emil Brunner's quote is reprinted in many church study resources including *Faith and Order: Toward a North American Conference-Study Guide* (Grand Rapids, Mich.: Eerdmans, 2005), p. 41.

Bill Graham's prayer was cited by Sandra Silberstein in *War of Words* (London: Routledge, 2002), p. 48.

The Sojourners' document "Deny Them Their Victory: A Religious Response to Terrorism" can be found on the National Council of Churches of Christ USA's Web site at http://www.ncccusa.org/news/interfaithstatement.html.

George W. Bush's comments about Islam as a religion of peace are quoted in the Pew Research Center publication *Lift Every Voice: A Report on Religion in American Public* Life (Washington, D.C.: Pew Research Center for People and the Press, 2002), p. 40. This document can be consulted at http://pewforum.org/publications/reports/lifteveryvoice.pdf.

Bush's pro-American cheer at Ground Zero on September 14, 2001, and other of his statements can be found in the CNN archives at http://archives.cnn.com/2001/US/09/14/bush.terrorism.

The NAE's position paper "For the Health of the Nation" (adopted October 7, 2004) can be found at http://www.nae.net/images/civic_responsibility2.pdf; the quotations are from page 11.

David Benke's participation in the post-9/11 "Prayer for America" at Yankee Stadium was cited as on the agenda for the Lutheran Church Missouri Synod's 2004 convention, posted at http://www.lcms.org/pages/internal.asp?NavID=4436.

Bill Maher's comments about religion were made during an appearance on *Scarborough Country*, MSNBC, February 15, 2005, http://www.msnbc.msn.com/id/6980984.

Ann Coulter's suggestions for combating terrorism were stated in her column "This Is War," posted on her Web site on September 12, 2001, http://www.anncoulter.org/columns/2001/091301.htm.

Jerry Falwell and Pat Robertson's statements were made during the September 13, 2001, broadcast of *The 700 Club*. A partial transcript from this show was posted on Beliefnet's Web site at http://www.beliefnet.com/story/87/story_8770_1.html.

The results from the Pew Research Center poll taken on September 19, 2001, documenting Americans' prayer lives after 9/11 are reported at http://people-press.org/reports/display.php3?PageID=30.

The text of the USA PATRIOT Act dated October 24, 2001, was obtained from the Library of Congress's Web site at http://thomas.loc.gov.

Amnesty International's study is posted at http://www.amnestyusa.org/racial_profiling/report/index.html.

Jerry Vines's comments about Islam were widely quoted, including the article "How Islam Bashing Got Cool," published by Beliefnet at http://www.beliefnet.com/story/110/story_11074_1.html.

Franklin Graham admitted in an interview on December 17, 2004, that right after the September 11 attacks, he called Islam evil. This interview was posted on Newsweek magazine's Web site at http://www.msnbc.msn.com/id/6730092/site/newsweek.

The pamphlet *Day the Terrorists Struck!* (McKeesport, Pa.: Beautiful Feet Publishing, 2002) was written by Jordan Armstrong.

The truly offensive pamphlet *Why?* (Riverside, Calif.: Harvest Ministries, 2001) was written by Greg Laurie.

Information about postdisaster resources produced by Episcopal Church related ministries can be obtained from http://www .episcopalmediacenter.org and http://www.trinitywallstreet.org.

The poem by child psychologist A. B. Curtiss is from her book *The Little Chapel That Stood* (Escondido, Calif.: Old Castle Publishing, 2003) and can be read online at http://www.abcurtiss.com/graphics/books2/l_chapel/little_chapel11.htm.

Diana Butler Bass's book *Broken We Kneel: Reflections on Faith and Citizenship* (San Francisco: Jossey-Bass) was published in 2004.

Information about the post-9/11 organizations identified by name in this chapter can be found at the following Web sites: http://www.artaid.org, http://www.911fallenheroes.org, http://www .firefamilytransport.org, and http://sjchapel.org.

C. S. Lewis is quoted from his book *Reflection on the Psalms* (New York: Harvest Books, 1964), p. 32.

The Iraq body count statistics are from iCasualties, "Iraq Coalition Casualty Count," November 24, 2005, posted at http://icasualties.org/oif.

George W. Bush's random reflections on war are from the following official White House press releases: "Guard and Reserves 'Define Spirit of America,'" September 17, 2001, http://www.whitehouse .gov/news/releases/2001/09/20010917-3.html; "Address to a Joint Session of Congress and the American People," September 19, 2001, http://www.whitehouse.gov/news/releases/2001/09/20010920-8 .html; "Remarks by the President on Home Ownership," June 18, 2002, http://www.whitehouse.gov/news/releases/2002/06/20020618-1 .html; "Interview of the President by Mouafac Harb of Middle East Television Network," January 29, 2004, http://www.whitehouse.gov/ news/releases/2004/02/20040218-10.html; "President's Remarks at an Ask the President Event," July 20, 2004, http://www.whitehouse .gov/news/releases/2004/07/20040720-7.html.; "President Signs Defense Bill," August 5, 2004, http://www.whitehouse.gov/news/ releases/2004/08/20040805-3.html; "Remarks by the President of

the American Legion," August 31, 2004, http://www.whitehouse
.gov/news/releases/2004/08/20040831-7.html; "President's Remarks
at Victory 2004 Luncheon," September 17, 2004, http://www
.whitehouse.gov/news/releases/2004/09/20040917-4.html; "Press Conference of the President," April 28, 2005, http://www.whitehouse
.gov/news/releases/2005/04/20050428-9.html; "President Discusses
Strengthening Social Security in Washington, D.C.," June 8, 2005,
http://www.whitehouse.gov/news/releases/2005/06/20050608-3
.html; "President Offers Condolences to People of London, Will
Not Yield to Terrorists," July 7, 2005, http://www.whitehouse.gov/
news/releases/2005/07/20050707-2.html; and "President Bush Meets
with President Torrijos of Panama," November 7, 2005, http://www
.whitehouse.gov/news/releases/2005/11/20051107.html.

The text of the letter "What We're Fighting For: A Letter from
America" is posted in many places on the Internet, including http://
www.usembassyjakarta.org/press_rel/colamitous_acts.html.

Jerry Falwell's comments relating to the war in Iraq were uttered
on the October 24, 2004, edition of CNN *Late Edition with Wolf
Blitzer*. A copy of this transcript can be found at http://cnnstudentnews
.CNN.com./TRANSCRIPTS/0410/24/le.01.html.

Sojourners' appeal to its readers to support our troops was sent to
subscribers of the weekly e-zine *Sojo.Mail* on May 18, 2005. A copy
of this e-mail can be found at http://www.sojo.net/index.cfm?action
=sojomail.display&issue=050518.

Chapter Three

G. K. Chesterton's quote is from *Illustrated London News*, April 9,
1924.

The transcript of Elizabeth Dole's remarks at the Republican
National Convention on August 31, 2004, was reprinted in the
Washington Post at http://www.washingtonpost.com/wp-dyn/articles/
A50426-2004Aug31.html.

That two million New Yorkers are at risk of going hungry every
night is stated by the Food Bank for New York City at www

.foodbanknyc.org/index.cfm?objectid=D995EE3A-3473-0E4E-CDC8A297A789EB12&flushcache=1&showdraft=1.

Barack Obama's keynote address was made on July 27, 2004, at the Democratic National Convention. A transcript of his speech was posted at the Democracy Now! Web site at http://www.democracynow.org/article.pl?sid=04/07/28/1313225.

The "Drum Circle, Peace Ritual, & Totally Tyranny-Free Party for the People" event was posted on a number of now defunct anti-RNC Web sites. The e-mail promoting this event is posted at http://lists.indymedia.org/pipermail/imc-nyc-photo/2004-August/0823-mm.html.

William Shakespeare's quote is from *Macbeth*, act 5, scene 5.

The text of Bob Jones's letter to George W. Bush following the November 2004 election was reprinted on the *Washington Post*'s Web site at http://www.washingtonpost.com/wp-dyn/content/article/2005/05/04/AR2005050402413_5.html.

Chapter Four

Rep. Don Davis's e-mail was reprinted in the *Charlotte Observer*, August 26, 2001, p. 2C.

Bill Clinton's sermon was delivered at Riverside Church in New York City on August 29, 2004. An excerpt of his remarks was published by Beliefnet at http://www.beliefnet.com/story/151/story_15194_1.html.

Bill Moyers's sermon was delivered at Riverside Church in New York City on October 4, 2004. An excerpt of his remarks was posted on the Bruderhof Community's Web site at http://www.bruderhof.com/articles/moyers-jesus.htm?source=DailyDig.

Brian McLaren's observations are from *A Generous Orthodoxy* (Grand Rapids, Mich.: Zondervan, 2004), pp. 83 and 295.

This description of Karl Barth's preaching style is reported in many places, including John R. W. Stott's book *Between Two Worlds* (Grand Rapids, Mich.: Eerdmans, 1992), p. 149.

David Buschman's comments are taken from his sermon "The Dirty Side of Leadership," preached on March 24, 2005, at the Princeton University Chapel. The sermon is posted online at http://web.princeton.edu/sites/chapel/Sermon%20Files/2005_ sermons/032405.htm.

Henri Nouwen's quote is from "Tempted to Replace Love with Power," in *Mornings with Henri J. M. Nouwen: Readings and Reflections* (Ann Arbor, Mich.: Servant Publications, 1997), p. 92.

Jimmy Carter's comment is from his book *Our Endangered Values: America's Moral Crisis* (New York: Simon & Schuster, 2005), p. 64.

Alan Storkey's book *Jesus and Politics: Confronting the Powers* (Grand Rapids, Mich.: Baker Books) was published in 2005.

Bill Press's comments are from his column "How Would Jesus Vote?" September 16, 2004, posted on his Web site at http://www .billpress.com/columns/091604.html.

Chapter Five

George W. Bush's observations on man and fish, delivered in Saginaw, Michigan, on September 29, 2000, have been documented in numerous news sources, included *The Guardian*, October 25, 2004, and posted at http://www.guardian.co.uk/fish/story/0,7369,1335341,00 .html.

Quotations regarding the Evangelical Environmental Network (EEN) in this chapter are from "On the Care of Creation: An Evangelical Declaration on the Care of Creation," available at http:// www.creationcare.org/resources/declaration.php, and the EEN's list of frequently asked questions at http://www.creationcare.org/responses/ faq.php.

Ecumenical Patriarch Bartholomew's comment and the NCC-CUSA's statement are from "God's Earth Is Sacred: An Open Letter to Church and Society in the United States," February 2005, posted at http://www.ncccusa.org/news/14.02.05theologicalstatement.html.

The Cree prophecy was quoted in "Government of Quebec Seeks to Divide Cree Nation and Foster Genocide," posted in 2002 on the First Nations Drum Web site, http://www.firstnationsdrum .com/Fall2002/EnviroJamesBay.htm.

The U.S. Catholic Bishops' statement is taken from their document "Faithful Citizenship: A Catholic Call to Political Responsibility," 2003, available at http://www.usccb.org/faithfulcitizenship/bishopStatement.html.

The NAE's position paper "For the Health of the Nation" (adopted October 7, 2004) can be found at http://www.nae.net/images/civic_responsibility2.pdf; the quotation is from pp. 11–12. Also, NAE president Ted Haggard spoke about his concerns that Christians care for the environment to Tom Brokaw on the NBC News special *In God They Trust*, which aired on October 25, 2005.

Jim Ball's and Tim LaHaye's perspectives on the need for Christians to care for the environment, a full recap of the Bill Moyers–James Watt tiff, and Ball's lengthy quotes on environmentalism and pollution are taken from Jim Ball's article "Ungodly Distortions: Evangelical Christians Know That Caring for God's Creation Is a Scriptural Imperative," published by Beliefnet at http://www.beliefnet.com/story/161/story_16141_1.html.

Mary Daly's statement is from her article "Sisterhood as Cosmic Covenant" in *Beyond God the Father: Toward a Philosophy of Women's Liberation* (Boston: Beacon Press, 1973), p. 178.

Exxon Mobil's campaign contributions were reported in "Business See Gain in GOP Takeover," *Washington Post*, March 27, 2005, p. A1. The article was also posted on the newspaper's Web site at http://www.washingtonpost.com/wp-dyn/articles/A3796-2005Mar26.html.

The plan to expand drilling in Alaska was reported by the Associated Press on January 23, 2004. A copy of this story was posted at http://www.azstarnet.com/dailystar/allheadlines/6957.php. Information on the history of the Arctic National Wildlife Refuge can be found on the U.S. Fish and Wildlife Service's Web site at http://arctic.fws.gov/faqs.htm.

Jim Ball's quote about global warning and the World Health Organization statistic noting how many people are affected by global warming are taken from Ball's article "A Christian Perspective on the Kyoto Protocol," February 16, 2005, posted at http://www.npr.org/templates/story/story.php?storyId=4500814.

The statistics on the consumption of fossil fuel resources in the United States is posted on information from the Population Institute at http://www.populationinstitute.org/teampublish/71_234_5215.cfm.

Senator Inhofe's remarks are taken from the article "Evangelicals Rethink Their Public Face," posted May 23, 2005, on MSNBC's Web site at http://msnbc.msn.com/id/7911488.

The Christian Sportsmen's Fellowship statement is from http://www.christiansportsman.com/about/about-mission.html#mission.

Karl Stoll's comments are taken from the article "Breaking Up Is Hard to Do," *Christianity Today*, April 2, 2001, posted at http://www.christianitytoday.com/ct/2001/005/13.26.html.

The WWJD (What Would Jesus Drive?) statement is from http://www.whatwouldjesusdrive.org/resources/fs_actions.pdf.

Andrew Greeley's commentary on SUVs is from his article "Global Warming Falsehoods: SUVs Are the Whipping Boy for a Natural Environmental Cycle," published by Beliefnet at http://www.beliefnet.com/story/85/story_8579_1.html.

The *Detroit News* reported the slump in SUV sales on September 2, 2005, on its Web site at http://www.detnews.com/2005/autosinsider/0509/02/A01-301633.htm.

JesusVeg.com's statement is taken from the frequently asked questions answered at http://www.jesusveg.com/qow999.html.

The Christian Vegetarian Association's mission statement can be found at http://www.christianveg.com/mission.htm.

Fletcher Harper's environmental observations are taken from phone conversations with him in July 2005 based on the materials posted on Greenfaith's Web site, http://www.greenfaith.org.

Maathai Wangari's quote is from "Fourth 'R' for Earth Day: Reduce, Reuse, Recycle, . . . Repair," *Christian Science Monitor*,

April 22, 2005, posted at http://www.christiansciencemonitor.com/
2005/0422/p09s01-coop.html.

Chapter Six

Heyward Carter's reflections on sexuality are from her interview
by Muffie Moroney, "And the Walls Came Tumbling Down," *Out-Smart*, Sept. 2001, posted at http://www.outsmartmagazine.com/
issue/i09-01/walls.html.

The FBI statistics are from "FBI Releases Hate Crime Statistics
for 2003," November 22, 2004, posted on the FBI's Web site at
http://www.fbi.gov/pressrel/pressrel04/pressrel112204.htm.

Pat Buchanan's reflections are from his column "Christianopho-
bia," dated December 13, 2004, and posted at *WorldNetDaily*, http://
www.worldnetdaily.com/news/article.asp?ARTICLE_ID=41900.

Joan Chittister's musings on Christ's ministry are from "Is
This Kind of Christianity Christian?" *National Catholic Reporter*,
February 17, 2005, posted at http://nationalcatholicreporter.org/
fwis/fw021705.htm.

The Episcopal Church, USA's declining numbers were reported
by CNN on August 6, 2003, at www.CNN.com/2003/US/08/05.

Chapter Seven

A transcript of Jerry Falwell's comments on *Meet the Press*,
November 28, 2004, can be found at http://www.msnbc.msn.com/
id/6601018.

Bush's comments as reported in *Ha'aretz* were quoted in the
Washington Post on June 27, 2003, p. A27.

Bob Woodward's reflections on Bush's mission are from his book
Bush at War (New York: Simon & Schuster, 2002), p. 67.

George W. Bush's comment that Jesus Christ is his favorite
philosopher was reported on the PBS program *Religion and Ethics* on
November 3, 2000. A transcript can be found at http://www.pbs.org/
wnet/religionandethics/week410/cover.html.

The U.S. Conference of Catholic Bishops' statement is from "Faithful Citizenship: A Catholic Call to Political Responsibility," 2003, posted at http://www.usccb.org/faithfulcitizenship/bishopStatement.html.

The text of the letter sent to Condoleezza Rice by church leaders on November 14, 2005, was posted at http://www.cmep.org/letters/2005Nov14_CMEP_Rice.htm.

Pat Robertson's reflections can be found in "Land of Israel: A Gift from God," posted on his Web site at http://www.patrobertson.com/teaching/TeachingonIsraelTerritory.asp.

That more than seven million Christians participated in Stand for Israel's International Day of Prayer was reported by *WorldNetDaily*, October 24, 2003, at http://www.worldnetdaily.com/news/article.asp?ARTICLE_ID=35234.

Excerpts from Adolf Hitler's speeches are from his book *My New Order*, edited by Raoul de Roussy de Sales (New York: Octagon Books, 1973), pp. 157 and 597.

"Ideologically Separated at Birth?" was published in *The Wittenburg Door* for March-April 1995.

The Council for National Policy's description of the organization's activities as noted on its 2000 IRS tax return was reported by ABC News on its Web site at http://abcnews.go.com/Politics/story?id=121170&page=1.

Chapter Eight

Joyce Meyer is quoted in Joe Conn, "The Christian Coalition: Born Again?" Americans United for the Separation of Church and State, posted in November 2002 at http://www.au.org/site/News2?page=NewsArticle&id=5492&abbr=cs.

The National Education Association's comment about prayer in the public schools is from "Guidance on Constitutionally Protected Prayer in Public Elementary and Secondary School," February 7, 2003, posted at http://www.ed.gov/policy/gen/guid/religionandschools/prayer_guidance.html.

George Carlin's comment on religion is from *When Will Jesus Bring the Pork Chops?* (New York: Hyperion, 2004), p. 18.

Warren Nord's quote is from "Teaching About Religion in the Public Schools: Where Do We Go from Here?" Pew Forum on Religion and Public Life, posted at http://pewforum.org/publications/reports/TeachingAboutReligion.pdf, p. 13.

The Bible aimed at teens is *Revolve: The Complete New Testament* (Nashville, Tenn.: Thomas Nelson Bibles, 2003).

Judge Dean is quoted in *Foolish Words: The Most Stupid Words Ever Spoken* (New York: Sterling Publishing Company, 2003), p. 62.

Steven Wright's comment is from *The Funny Pages* (Kansas City, Mo.: Andrews McMeel, 2002), p. 88.

Tim LaHaye spoke in an interview by Chris Fabry, host of the radio program *First Edition*, that was posted in March 2004 at http://www.faithfulreader.com/authors/au-lahaye-tim.asp.

Kenneth R. Miller's reflections are from his book *Finding Darwin's God* (New York: HarperCollins, 1999), p. 291.

George W. Bush's comments on teaching intelligent design in the public schools were published in the *Washington Post* on August 3, 2005, p. A1.

The statement by the Intelligent Design Network, a Kansas-based nonprofit organization that seeks institutional objectivity in origins science, can be found at http://www.intelligentdesignnetwork.org.

Kurt Vonnegut Jr. was quoted in London's *Observer* newspaper on December 27, 1987.

Pat Robertson rebuked the town of Dover on *The 700 Club* on November 10, 2005.

Chapter Nine

Stanley Hauerwas's comment is from "Abortion Theologically Understood," February 1991, posted at http://lifewatch.org/abortion.html.

Carlton V. Veazey's quote is from "On the Brink of Theocracy," May 5, 2005, posted at http://www.americanprogress.org/site/pp.asp?c=biJRJ8OVF&b=667491.

The March for Women's Lives service sponsored by the Religious Coalition for Reproductive Choice held on April 28, 2004, was reported by the Shalom Center at http://www.shalomctr.org/node/585.

The statistic citing that more than one-third of the children in the United States live in low-income families is from the National Center for Children in Poverty at www.nccp.org/pub_cpf04.html.

Roe v. *Wade* (410 U.S. 113) was decided in 1973.

The Catholic Task Force statement is from the Catholics for Choice press release "Catholic Bishops Called On to Repudiate Republican Claim That GOP Positions Are 'Closest' to Catholic Church's," April 13, 2000, posted at http://www.catholicsforchoice.org/new/pressrelease/041300RepublicanClaim.htm.

Joan Chittister's reflections are from her column "I Give Up: Who Stole the Rest of the Commandments?" *National Catholic Reporter*, November 26, 2004, which can be read at http://nationalcatholicreporter.org/fwis/pc112604.htm.

Patrick J. Mahoney's comments are from "Frist Backs Stem Cell Research, Angers Abortion Foes," CNN, August 2, 2005, reprinted at http://www.cnn.com/2005/POLITICS/07/29/frist.stem.cells.ap.

Jesse Jackson's comments are from "Rev. Jesse Jackson's Statement on Terri Schiavo's Fight for Life," Beliefnet, March 25, 2005, posted at http://www.beliefnet.com/story/163/story_16349_1.html.

John Shelby Spong's comments are from "Assisted Suicide: A Christian Choice and a New Freedom," Beliefnet, posted at http://www.beliefnet.com/story/121/story_12143_1.html.

The statistic noting $237 million spent by health lobbyists in the year 2000 is cited in Janice Hopkins Tanne, "U.S. Healthcare Lobbyists Outspend Other Pressure Groups," *BMJ*, April 3, 2004, and credited to the *American Journal of Medicine*, 2004, *116*, 474–477.

The second edition of *The Common Ground Network for Life and Choice Manual*, by Mary Jacksteit and Adrienne Kaufmann (Washington, D.C.: Search for Common Ground, 1999), can be consulted at http://www.sfcg.org/programmes/us/pdf/manual.pdf.

Chapter Ten

Jesus CEO: Using Ancient Wisdom for Visionary Leadership (New York: Hyperion, 1996) is by Laura Beth Jones. *God Is My CEO: Following God's Principles in a Bottom-Line World* (Cincinnati, Ohio: Adams Media, 2001) is by Larry S. Julian.

Joel Osteen, televangelist and senior pastor of the thirty-thousand-member Lakewood Church in Houston, Texas, the largest congregation in America, was quoted by Laura Sheahen in " 'Expect God's Favor': Interview with Joel Osteen" at the Beliefnet Web site, http://www.beliefnet.com/story/157/story_15735_1.html.

For information on the Episcopal church's real estate holdings in New York City, see http://www.trinitywallstreet.org and http://www.trinityrealestate.org. The Episcopal News Service reported that Trinity's real estate holdings were approximately six million square feet in a release titled "Downtown Leader Carl Weisbrod Named New Head of Trinity Real Estate," posted May 10, 2005, at http://www.episcopalchurch.org/3577_61872_ENG_HTM.htm.

Mike Yaconelli's warning about equating God with Santa Claus is from *Tough Faith: The Search for Honest, Durable Christianity* (Chicago: Cook, 1976), as excerpted in Mike Yaconelli, *Selected Writings* (El Cajon, Calif.: Youth Specialties, 2003), p. 16.

Thich Nhat Hanh's fourteen precepts are presented in *Interbeing: Fourteen Guidelines for Engaged Buddhism* (Berkeley, Calif.: Parallax Press, 1987), p. 20.

Thomas Keating's commentaries on the story of the widow's mite are taken from his book *Crisis of Faith/Crisis of Love* (New York: Continuum, 1995), pp. 77 and 82.

George W. Bush's comments about feeding the hungry are taken from a White House press release titled, "President Bush Discusses Faith-Based Initiatives with Urban Leaders," July 16, 2003, posted on the White House Web site at http://www.whitehouse.gov/news/releases/2003/07/20030716-2.html.

The NAE's position paper "For the Health of the Nation" (adopted October 7, 2004) can be found at http://www.nae.net/images/civic_responsibility2.pdf; the quotations are from pp. 8 and 9.

The letter signed by more than eighty evangelical leaders stressing six social issues that should shape voters' decisions in the 2004 election is referenced in the article "Christian Leaders Take a Stand for Morality in Election," posted October 8, 2004, on the Focus on the Family Web site at http://www.family.org/welcome/press/a0034054.cfm.

The results of the Alliance to End Hunger/Call to Renewal survey of voter's concerns was posted March 2, 2004, at http://www.alliancetoendhunger.org/articles/2004/rns_mar_2.htm.

Jim Wallis's comments about George W. Bush and the Sermon on the Mount are from his interview in *Mother Jones*, March 10, 2005.

Martin Luther King's comments are from the sermon "Beyond Vietnam: A Time to Break Silence," delivered on April 4, 1967, at Riverside Church in New York City.

The poverty statistics cited, as well as the mention of the One Table, Many Voices conference, are from the Center for Public Justice's 2005 report "Hunger No More," posted at http://www.cpjustice.org/pjr/2005_3Q_IssueBrief.

Ronald J. Sider's seminal book *Rich Christians in an Age of Hunger: A Biblical Study* (Downers Grove, Ill.: InterVarsity Press) was published in 1977. His comments on the U.S. government's failure to address poverty are from an interview with *World Magazine*, May 14, 2005, posted at http://www.worldmag.com/subscriber/displayarticle.cfm?id=10623.

Jim Wallis's critiques about the Bush administration's "unbiblical" budget and faith-based initiatives are from "The Things That Make for Peace," *Sojourners*, July-August 2003, posted at http://www.sojo.net/index.cfm?action=magazine.article&issue=soj0307&article=030751. His book *God's Politics* (San Francisco: HarperSanFrancisco, 2005) offers in-depth reflections of Wallis's approach to the role that religion can play in the political sphere.

Joan Chittister's reflections on the budget are from her column "Is This Kind of Christianity Christian?" published in *National Catholic Reporter*, February 17, 2005, and posted at http://nationalcatholicreporter.org/fwis/fw021705.htm.

The letter sent to President George W. Bush by religious leaders, dated December 23, 2002, was posted on the Episcopal Public Policy Network's Web site at http://www.episcopalchurch.org/3654_13573_ENG_HTM.htm. The letter Bush received from five mainline Protestant leaders, dated April 28, 2005, was posted on the Center for American Progress's Web site at http://www.americanprogress.org/atf/cf/{E9245FE4-9A2B-43C7-A521-5D6FF2E06E03}/Denomination_statement_post_conf.pdf.

The Budget of the President, dated February 7, 2005, was posted on the Office of Management and Budget's Web site at http://www.whitehouse.gov/omb/budget/fy2006/message.html.

A brief analysis of Bush's FY 2006 budget was prepared by the Democratic staff of the Senate Budget Committee on February 8, 2005. A copy of this analysis can be obtained from http://budget.senate.gov/democratic/press/2005/bushfy06budgetbriefanalysis0208051.pdf.

The letter sent to President Bush by Richard Land, Jim Wallis, and other evangelical leaders dated January 17, 2005, was posted on the Evangelicals for Social Action's Web site at http://www.esa-online.org/pdfs/bushletter.pdf.

Mother Teresa's comment is from her book *No Greater Love* (Novato, Calif.: New World Library, 1997), p. 29.

The statements about ending hunger are taken from the Bread for the World's Web site at http://www.bread.org.

Chapter Eleven

George W. Bush's "Words from the President on Prayer" were posted on July 21, 2005, on the Presidential Prayer Team Web site, http://www.presidentialprayerteam.org. His comments on religion were made during a White House press conference on April 28, 2005, and posted on the White House Web site at http://www.whitehouse.gov/news/releases/2005/04/20050428-9.html.

James Dobson's comments on religious plurality are from "Dr. Dobson Reflects on a Changed Nation," posted on the Focus on the Family's Web site at http://www.family.org/welcome/press/a0017797.cfm.

Thomas Paine's religious lament is found in his book *Age of Reason*, originally published in 1794.

Mike Yaconelli's quote is from *Messy Spirituality* (El Cajon, Calif.: Youth Specialties, 2002), p. 49.

Stephen L. Carter's commentary on the East Waynesville Baptist Church's fracas is from his article "First Things First," *Christianity Today*, July 20, 2005, posted at http://www.christianitytoday.com/ct/2005/007/30.54.html.

The quotations attributed to Daniel Homan and Lonni Collins Pratt are from their book *Radical Hospitality: Benedict's Way of Love* (Orleans, Mass.: Paraclete Press, 2002), pp. xxix–xxx, 64–65, and 70.

Brian McLaren's observation is from his book *A Generous Orthodoxy* (Grand Rapids, Mich.: Zondervan, 2004), p. 140.

Dietrich Bonhoeffer's comments are taken from *A Testament to Freedom: The Essential Writings of Dietrich Bonhoeffer* (New York: HarperCollins, 1990), p. 319.

Henri Nouwen's quote is from his book *Reaching Out* (New York: Doubleday, 1975), p. 71.

Tom Lehrer's lines are from "National Brotherhood Week" (copyright © 1965 Tom Lehrer), from his album *That Way the Year That Was* (Reprise Records, 1965).

Madeleine L'Engle's quote is taken from her interview in *The Wittenburg Door*, March-April 2000, p. 37.

The Chesterton quote is from *What's Wrong with the World* (New York: Dodd, Mead, 1910), p. 48.

Miroslav Volf's reflections are from *Free of Charge: Giving and Forgiving in a Culture Stripped of Grace* (Grand Rapids, Mich.: Zondervan, 2006), p. 131.

Kinky Friedman's statement was uttered during his appearance at the Texas Book Festival and broadcast on Book-TV, November 5, 2005.

The song "Jesus Loves Me but He Can't Stand You," © 1991 by Don Peters, is from the Austin Lounge Lizards CD *Lizard Vision Live* (Flying Fish Records, 1992) and is featured on the DVD *Lizards Times Twenty* (Blue Corn Music, 2004). The lyrics are reprinted with the permission of Don Peters.

Chapter Twelve

Thomas Jefferson's musings on religion were quoted by Charles B. Sanford in *The Religious Life of Thomas Jefferson* (Charlottesville: University of Virginia Press, 1984), p. 13.

The retelling of Karl Barth's 1962 trip to America was posted on the *Christianity Today* Web site at http://www.christianitytoday .com/history/special/131christians/barth.html.

C. S. Lewis's reflections are from *The Four Loves* (London: Harvest/Harcourt Brace, 1960).

Peter Kreeft gave his reflections on agape during "The Question of God," part two of the PBS program *C. S. Lewis: The Four Loves*. The transcript can be read at http://www.pbs.org/wgbh/questionofgod/ transcript/four.html.

Steve Chalke and Alan Mann's words are from *The Lost Message of Jesus* (Grand Rapids, Mich.: Zondervan, 2003), pp. 86 and 94.

Jim Wallis's reflections are from *The Call to Conversion*, rev. ed. (San Francisco: HarperSanFrancisco, 2005), p. 112.

David P. Gushee and Dennis P. Hollinger's commentary is from their essay "Toward an Evangelical Ethical Methodology," featured in *Toward an Evangelical Public Policy* (Grand Rapids, Mich.: Baker Books, 2005), p. 138

Mary Stevenson's poem "Footprints in the Sand" was written in 1936 but copyrighted only in 1984; see http://www.footprints-inthe- sand.com.

Archbishop Desmond Tutu's reflections are from his book *God Has a Dream* (New York: Doubleday, 2004), p. 3.

Mike Yaconelli's reflections are from "The Safety of Fear," originally published in *The Wittenburg Door* and excerpted in Mike Yaconelli, *Selected Writings* (El Cajon, Calif.: Youth Specialties, 2003), pp. 9–10.

Stanley Hauerwas's words are from an interview posted on Homiletics Online at http://www.homileticsonline.com/subscriber/ interviews/hauerwas.asp.

Sanctuary worship is described at http://www.sanctuaryny.org.

Gerald May's quote is from "The Vision and the Path," *Shalem News On Line*, Fall 1996, posted at http://archives.shalem.org/sn/20.3gm.html.

Epilogue

Lenny Bruce's comment on religion is from his monologue "Christ and Moses," published in *The Big Book of Jewish Humor* (New York: HarperCollins, 1980), p. 215.

Flannery O'Connor's *Wise Blood* (New York: Harcourt Brace) was first published in 1952.

John Dear's quote is taken from his article "Pharisee Nation," dated February 15, 2005, which was posted on the Common Dreams Web site at http://www.commondreams.org/views05/0215-21.htm.

Michael Lerner's quote is from *The Left Hand of God* (San Francisco: HarperSanFrancisco, 2006), p. 2.

The Network of Spiritual Progressives core vision statement is posted at http://www.spiritualprogressives.org.

Information about the NCCCUSA and its "For the Peace of the World: A Christian Curriculum on International Relations" can be found at http://www.ncccusa.org/peace.

Gandhi's reflections on Christianity are found in Stanley E. Jones, *Christ of the Indian Road* (Whitefish, Mont.: Kessinger, 2003), pp. 126–127; the book was originally published in 1925.

Appendix B

Portions of this timeline appeared in Robert Darden, ed., *And on the Eighth Day God Laughed* (North Richland Hills, Tex.: Bibal Press, 2002).

Dick Morris's report of Bill Clinton's 1995 spiritual awakening is from an interview published in *The Wittenburg Door*, November-December 1997.

Acknowledgments

Although I always find acknowledgments to be more than a bit sappy, this book could not have happened had it not been for the people who have served as guides over the years as I continue along this admittedly crooked spiritual path. First, I want to thank my family for any encouragement they have offered, especially my grandparents, the late Roy and Ruby Clogston. They showed me what unconditional love is when I needed it the most. I need to thank my teachers—James Dodding, for being the first person who really believed in me and ignited my creative spark; Carol Fox Prescott, for showing me how to breathe and be in the moment; Gary Austin, for teaching me the joy of creating new material through the spirit of improv; and Wenndy MacKenzie, for giving life to my voice.

Kudos to my fellow Christians, who worshiped with me at St. Bart's 9 o'clock service during the '80s, everyone I met during Habitat for Humanity's Jimmy Carter Work Project 2000, and the staff and volunteers with the Emergency Disaster Services for the Salvation Army of Greater New York. You have shown me what "church" can be—the reality that we can be "the universal church" gives me great hope despite what appears at times to be insurmountable obstacles. Thanks to my comrades and professors at Yale Divinity School for helping me refine and shape my theology and get my head out of the Ivy League towers and into the world.

I would like to thank the late Mike Yaconelli for buying my first article, "Beavis and Butt-head Are Saved" (*The Wittenburg Door*,

March-April 1994), and getting me started on this crazy writing journey; Robert Darden for his expert editorial guidance over the years; my agent, Giles Anderson, for his diligence and kindness in seeing this project to fruition; Carol Hobbs for transcribing my *Door* interviews over the years; Rebecca Hoe Lopez for being another pair of eyes when I needed them; and Julianna Gustafson, Catherine Craddock, and Andrea Flint at Jossey-Bass and Marcia Ford for their expert editorial guidance in shepherding this book to publication.

And I reserve a special thank-you for those generous souls who offered me considerable guidance in shaping this book but have asked that I not thank them publicly—may they someday have the courage to preach in public what they whispered to me in private.

—B.G.

About the Author

Becky Garrison serves as Senior Contributing Editor for *The Wittenburg Door*, the oldest, largest, and only religious satire magazine in the United States. Her additional writing credits include work for the *New York Times*, the *Tonight Show*, Stackpole Books, Bibal Press, Relevantmagazine.com, Sojo.net, *Episcopal Life*, *The Living Church*, *Prism*, *SoMA: A Review of Religion and Culture*, *American Angler*, *Game and Fish Magazine*, *Fly Fish America*, *Sailing*, *Oxygen* magazine, *Fly Fishing in Saltwaters*, Fly Anglers Online, flyfish.com, and Sportsology.net. She has master's degrees in divinity and in social work from Yale University and Columbia University, respectively, and an undergraduate degree in theater arts from Wake Forest University. She is currently working with Gary Austin, founder of the Groundlings, the legendary Los Angeles improv company, on a memoir focusing on the connections between alcoholism, fishing, sailing, and religion.